British Concentration Camps

A Brief History: From 1900-1975

This book is dedicated to my father, Victor Webb, from whom I first heard the story of the Polish concentration camps in Scotland

British Concentration Camps

A Brief History: From 1900-1975

Simon Webb

PEN & SWORD HISTORY

First published in Great Britain in 2016 by
Pen & Sword History
an imprint of
Pen & Sword Books Ltd
47 Church Street
Barnsley
South Yorkshire
S70 2AS

ISBN 9781473846296

Typeset in 11.5 pt Ehrhardt MT by
Replika Press Pvt Ltd, India
Printed and bound in the UK by
CPI UK

Pen & Sword Books Ltd incorporates the imprints of Pen & Sword
Archaeology, Atlas, Aviation, Battleground, Discovery, Family
History, History, Maritime, Military, Naval, Politics, Railways, Select,
Social History, Transport, True Crime, and Claymore Press, Frontline
Books, Leo Cooper, Praetorian Press, Remember When,
Seaforth Publishing and Wharncliffe.

For a complete list of Pen & Sword titles please contact
PEN & SWORD BOOKS LIMITED
47 Church Street, (Barnsley: South Yorkshire, S70 2AS, England
E-mail: enquiries@pen-and-sword.co.uk
Website: www.pen-and-sword.co.uk

Contents

List of Plates

Introduction

History, it is often said, is written by the victors. Nowhere is the truth of this aphorism more neatly demonstrated than in the probable reaction of many readers to the title of this book. For most people in Europe and America, the very expression 'concentration camp' is inextricably linked to the horrors of the Third Reich; mention of concentration camps invariably conjuring up images of Auschwitz and Dachau. From this perspective, the words 'British concentration camp' appear strange, almost oxymoronic. It was not always so. In fact it is only since the end of the Second World War, and the allied victory over Nazi Germany, that concentration camps and Germany have become associated in this way.

It might help to break this strong mental association of one particular country's use of such camps if we look now at Plate 1, which shows a newspaper headline from a century ago. It is from the *Manchester Guardian* of 4 December 1914 and reads: 'DISORDER AT LANCASTER CONCENTRATION CAMP'. There is something oddly disconcerting about such a headline; it looks more as though it might be from some dystopian fantasy about the future, rather than a relic of Britain's past. It should be remembered that this was not a prisoner of war camp, but held only civilians. In other words, it really was a concentration camp.

Before looking briefly at one or two other examples of the kind of establishments which will be examined in this book, perhaps it should be pointed out that order at concentration camps of the kind mentioned in the above newspaper headline was maintained in the most ferocious manner. The 'disorder' at Lancaster Concentration Camp was dealt with by a bayonet charge against unarmed civilians. On 19 November that same year, protests at another concentration camp on the Isle of Man resulted in troops firing volleys of shots at the inmates, killing six of them. Among the dead were two men who had, until three months earlier, been working as waiters in hotels.

Having considered one instance of concentration camps operating in Britain a hundred years ago, perhaps a few more examples might be helpful in showing that such camps were being operated either in the United Kingdom or by the British army overseas for much of the twentieth century.

- In 1901 and 1902 more than 22,000 children under the age of sixteen died of starvation and disease in concentration camps run by the British army.
- Moscow radio and the Soviet newspaper *Pravda* claimed in 1945 that Britain had allowed the Polish government in exile to establish a number of concentration camps in Scotland, where the prisoners were predominantly communists and Jews. These statements turned out to be quite correct.
- Although the use of slave labour had been defined during the Nuremberg trials as a crime against humanity, in 1946 a fifth of Britain's agricultural labourers were effectively slaves, held in a network of closely guarded camps. The following year, 25 per cent of the land workforce in Britain was provided by this same forced labour.
- In 1972, almost 1,000 political prisoners in the United Kingdom were being held behind barbed wire at a former RAF base. Some of these men would spend years being detained without any right to a trial. The European Commission on Human Rights ruled that a number of them had been subjected to torture.

Before going any further, it might be helpful to define just what we mean by concentration camps and to examine the difference between concentration camps *per se* and the extermination camps run by the Nazis at locations in Poland such as Treblinka and Sobibor.

Here are two definitions of the expression 'concentration camp', drawn at random from books in the reference department of the local lending library. The first, from the 2003 edition of the *Compact Oxford English Dictionary*, tells us that a concentration camp is a 'camp for detaining political prisoners'. The second, from the 2005 edition of *Brewer's Dictionary of Phrase and Fable*, says that a concentration camp is 'A guarded camp for non-military (usually political) prisoners'. In neither of these definitions is there the suggestion that concentration camps are places where the inmates are massacred or even badly mistreated. This misunderstanding of the essential nature of concentration camps, that they were somehow associated with genocide, arose after the end of the Second World War, when newsreels at the cinema showed ghastly scenes from German camps such as Belsen, where many had died in the later stages of the war. Now Belsen was an example of a very badly run and cruelly administered concentration camp, but its primary purpose was never the murder of inmates. The many deaths there were an incidental outcome; precipitated by gross overcrowding and other exceptional circumstances.

Later on, when information about camps such as Auschwitz became available, concentration camps began to be associated with mass killing in gas chambers. This was because in addition to the concentration camp at Auschwitz, there was also a killing installation. The two parts of the camp were separate though, and the idea that concentration camps as such were part of the systematic destruction of the enemies of the Third Reich is quite mistaken. The aim of concentration camps is to hold prisoners securely; the aim of death camps is to dispose of prisoners as they arrive. These are two quite different types of establishment.

After the end of the Second World War, it was said that of all the misleading Nazi propaganda, no lie was more successful than the one which suggested that concentration camps were an invention of the British and that the Germans had only developed and expanded a concept which had its roots in the British Empire. The idea that the British invented concentration camps was sedulously peddled during the 1930s by the leaders of the Third Reich. In February 1939, for example, Sir Nevile Henderson, British ambassador to Germany, had a meeting with Hermann Goering. In the course of their encounter in Berlin, Henderson denounced the 'loathsome and detestable brutalities' taking place in concentration camps such as Dachau and Buchenwald. For answer, Goering went to a bookshelf and took down the volume of a German encyclopaedia covering the letter

'K' and showed the ambassador the entry for 'Konzentrationslager', which began; 'First used by the British in the South African War...'

Throughout the 1930s, Minister for Propaganda Josef Goebbels had also fostered the notion that concentration camps were a British invention. Postcards purporting to show the grim conditions in the camps run by the British during the Boer war were circulated. A film, *Om Paul*, was subsidised by the German government. This historical drama about the Boer War suggested that the British army had devised and operated the first concentration camps.

For many years after the war, this 'myth' of the British invention of concentration camps was widely treated as being a classic example of German propaganda; the big lie. In retrospect though, it appears that if anything the British involvement in developing and promoting the use of concentration camps was even more widespread and extensive than even Goering and Goebbels had claimed. Perhaps a few instances might make this clear.

The opening of Dachau on 22 March 1933, the first of the German concentration camps, was eerily foreshadowed by the establishment of a concentration camp in a remote part of Britain seventeen years earlier. Like Dachau, this camp was established around a disused factory and was intended to take enemies of the state from the general prison system and concentrate them in one place. To take another example, one of the most notorious incidents in Nazi Germany was the event in 1938 which became known as 'Krystalnacht' or the 'Night of Broken Glass'. The shops and business premises of those seen as enemies of the state were looted and destroyed by rampaging mobs. The victims of this pogrom, far from being protected by the police, were themselves arrested and marched off to *schutzhaft* or 'protective custody' in concentration camps. This event too was eerily similar to what had happened in the English port city of Liverpool in 1915.

A recurring theme in this book will be the uncanny way in which the concentration camp system of the Third Reich seemed to echo the kind of thing which had either happened in this country or been organised by the British abroad. We shall be examining this idea by looking at concentration camps and similar establishments run either in the United

Kingdom itself or by the British army abroad. Most of these camps were directly administered by the British, although one group of concentration camps which were operating in Britain during the Second World War were run by the Polish army, but with the encouragement and permission of the British government.

Although the British were instrumental in developing and refining the concept of the concentration camp, they did not actually *invent* them. Ironically, and not withstanding Goebbels' propaganda, the very first concentration camps which were known by that name had nothing at all to do with Britain. They were set up at the end of the nineteenth century by a general of German descent.

Chapter One

1896
A Prussian General's Idea: The Origin and Nature of Concentration Camps

The British may have pioneered the concept of concentration camps but it was a German who actually invented the concentration camp. Valeriano Weyler y Nicolau, born in 1838, was the son of a Prussian. His father was a career soldier who had moved to Spain and Valeriano decided to follow in his footsteps; becoming a lieutenant in the Spanish army by the age of twenty. His was a glittering military career. He fought in the Ten-Years War (1868-78), and was later appointed Captain-General of the Canary Islands. It was an earlier incident in his life though, when as a young man he had been sent to Washington as the military attache at the Spanish embassy, that gave Valeriano Wyler the idea for which he was to attain fame or, perhaps more accurately, notoriety.

During the American Civil War, while he was attached to the embassy in Washington, young Weyler heard about the tactics employed by General William Sherman, as he swept through the southern states using what would later become known as a 'scorched earth' policy. Not only was Sherman an exponent of brutal warfare, burning entire towns to terrify the enemy into submission, he also waged a campaign which some thought amounted to genocide against the Indians. Using as his slogan, 'The only good Indian is a dead one', Sherman harried the Indians mercilessly; seeing that they were penned up in camps where they died from starvation and illness. Sherman's activities, both against the Confederacy and the Indians, made a great and lasting impression upon the young soldier who went on to govern several Spanish colonies.

At the age of 58, *General* Weyler as he was by then, was sent to Cuba to suppress, by any means he chose, the rebellion which was threatening to drive the Spanish from the island nation. When he arrived in Cuba as the newly appointed governor of the colony, Weyler found that the rebels were practically at the gates of Havana, the capital. He realised that only an altogether new and radical policy would be able to save the country for Spain.

The expression 'concentration camps' might only date from the end of the nineteenth and beginning of the twentieth centuries, but the concept itself is an ancient one. In 1997, an archaeologist working at Hadrian's Wall even suggested that evidence had been found of the world's earliest concentration camp, which had been set up in Britain! The foundations of many round huts were found near a Roman fort and the idea was mooted that this had been some sort of camp under the control of the Roman army and holding British hostages.

More recently, camps such as Andersonville in Georgia, a prisoner of war camp during the American Civil War, have produced conditions as shocking as any seen in the twentieth century. Of the 45,000 Union prisoners sent to Andersonville, no fewer than 13,000 died of starvation and disease. The commandant of the camp was hanged after the war. Most of the previous camps that were established before the Cuban War, places like Andersonville, were specifically for prisoners who had been fighting against an army or working to overthrow a regime. What was novel about the camps set up by General Weyler was that they were, from the very beginning, intended to house civilian non-combatants; primarily women and children who had no part in any fighting.

The main problem faced by the Spanish army in Cuba was that the guerrillas fighting them were all but indistinguishable from the ordinary Cuban peasants who were working the land. These men could ambush a Spanish column and then slip back to their homes later and resume their normal life; which meant that the enemy had no need to worry about supplies and so on. They just went home at the end of the action, to wives who had a hot meal ready and waiting for them. It was clear that unusual action would be needed and unconventional tactics would have to be devised to combat this new type of belligerent.

The idea that General Weyler came up with was to clear the countryside of its inhabitants and force the entire population into villages and towns. These would then be fortified and defended against the rebels. Anybody found in the countryside would be automatically viewed as an insurgent and liable to be shot down without warning. The fertile fields themselves would be untended and the peasants confined to the towns left to provide for themselves as best they were able.

On 21 October 1896, General Weyler announced:

All the inhabitants of the country now outside the line of fortifications of the towns, shall within the period of eight days concentrate themselves in the town so occupied by the troops.

The homes that the peasants left behind were frequently destroyed and their farms ravaged so that they could not provide food for the rebels. The temporary camps set up within the towns were only ever intended to be a stopgap measure. No real provision was made for those within them. As the months passed, conditions grew increasingly desperate.

To get some idea of the conditions of these 'reconcentrados', as the Spanish called those whom they had concentrated in this way, we cannot do better than examine the evidence of an eyewitness. United States Senator Redfield Proctor, from Vermont, visited Cuba to see for himself what was happening in the country. On 17 March 1898, he gave a speech in the US Senate, describing what he had found during his stay:

It is not peace, nor is it war. It is desolation and distress, misery and starvation. Every town and village is surrounded by a trocha (trench) a sort of rifle pit, but constructed on a plan new to me, the dirt being thrown up on the inside and a barbed wire fence on the outer side of the trench. These trochas have at every corner, and at frequent intervals along the sides, what are there called forts, but which are really small block-houses, many of them more like a large sentry box, loop-holed for musketry, and with a guard of from two to ten soldiers in each. The purpose of these trochas is to keep reconcentrados in as well as to keep the insurgents out.

> *From all the surrounding country the people have been driven into these fortified towns and held there to subsist as they can. They are virtually prison yards and not unlike one in general appearance, except that the walls are not so-high and strong, but they suffice, where every point is in range of a soldier's rifle, to keep in the poor reconcentrado women and children.*

With no crops to harvest in the towns and no livestock, the situation for the hundreds of thousands of smallholders and peasants who were thus confined in this way was dire indeed.

What Weyler called his, 'Reconstruction Plan' may have been a military success, but it soon became a humanitarian disaster. Well over a quarter of a million people died of hunger or disease as a direct consequence of Weyler's actions in setting up his camps for 'reconcentrados'. One figure for the total number of dead is 321,934.

World reaction to the campaign led by General Weyler was wholly unfavourable; except of course in Spain itself. There, Weyler was regarded by Conservatives as a saviour of the nation. What could not be denied was that faced with a new kind of warfare, the general had come up with a novel tactic; one which would become enormously widespread in the new century which was about to dawn. Scorched earth policies, the destruction of homes and herding of civilians into captivity behind barbed wire fences might have been a novelty at the end of the nineteenth century, but it was to be anything but out-of-the-ordinary by the time that the twentieth century ended. Indeed, the concentration camp, as used by Nazi Germany, Soviet Russia, communist China and Britain bids fair to be regarded as something of a *leit motif* for the entire century. From the time of General Weyler onwards, civilians were frequently regarded as legitimate targets during times of war. Rather than, as was previously the case, being seen as largely an irrelevance, non-combatants were now viewed as pawns to be used and abused as circumstances dictated.

One nation above all others though, looked with interest at the exploits of General Weyler and his unorthodox methods for subduing an elusive enemy. It was this nation which was to adopt the idea of concentration camps from the first year of the twentieth century, and continue to use them, more or less continuously, right through to the middle of the 1970s. Only a few years after the Cuban War, the British found themselves facing a precisely similar situation of their own in southern Africa. It was perhaps inevitable that they would seek to adopt similar means to the Spanish when they came to tackle a guerrilla war of their own; one which almost defeated the mightiest empire the world had ever seen.

Chapter Two

1900-1902
Lord Kitchener's Genocide: 'Methods of Barbarism' in the Boer War

T he word 'genocide' was unknown in 1900. It was Raphael Lemkin, a Polish lawyer, who coined the expression in 1943, feeling that the murderous activities of the Nazis in Eastern Europe were so extraordinary that existing words were simply not adequate to describe what had been going on in Poland and Russia during the early years of the Second World War. The word may be relatively new, but the concept of systematically exterminating an entire nation or race is at least as old as recorded history. The Bible, for example, tells us in the Book of Joshua that when the Children of Israel entered the land of Canaan, they were commanded by God to kill all the existing inhabitants of the country. Every man, woman and child living in Jericho, the first city conquered by the Hebrews, was put to the sword and the city burned to the ground. Only one family escaped this holocaust.

The decimation or destruction of a people or tribe in this way may sometimes be accomplished by cold-blooded murder, but the same end can be obtained by producing living conditions which lead to starvation and death from disease. This happened of course in the nineteenth century, with the native Americans living under the jurisdiction of the United States. In 1945, the civilised world was shocked to see the conditions in German concentration camps such as Belsen, whose inmates had died in their tens of thousands from malnutrition and epidemics of illnesses such as typhoid. This too was genocide and was officially recognised as such in 1948, when the United Nations defined genocide as, 'any of the following acts committed with the intent to destroy, in whole or in part, a national, ethnic, racial or religious group, as such'. The UN

Convention on Genocide then went on to specify, apart from outright killing, 'Deliberately inflicting on the group conditions of life calculated to bring about its physical destruction in whole or part'.

Before we examine in detail the network of concentration camps set up by the British in the opening years of the twentieth century in, it has since been claimed, an effort to destroy a national group in this way, perhaps we should look at Plates 2 and 3. Belsen was mentioned above and at first glance, these images could very well have originated from events at that most infamous of concentration camps. In fact, both are from 1901; some forty-two years before Belsen opened its gates. The first is a French cartoon, designed to draw attention to the horrors of the British concentration camps in South Africa. The second is of a child from Bloemfontein Concentration Camp; one of the worst of the camps. Seven-year-old Lizzie van Zuyl and her family were deliberately starved by the British soldiers controlling the concentration camp in which they were detained. Lizzie was on the point of dying of malnutrition, when she contracted typhoid and died on 9 May 1901. Her fate was precisely the same as Anne Frank and many others who died in Belsen almost half a century later.

Before looking in detail at the concentration camps organised by the British in the opening years of the last century, it will first be necessary to set the scene by asking ourselves what the British were doing in southern Africa in the late nineteenth and early twentieth centuries. Most people in Britain have heard of the Boer War; few have any clear idea what it was all about.

The first European colony in South Africa was established by the Dutch East India Company in 1652. By the late eighteenth century, this outpost on the southern tip of Africa was looking very attractive to the British, who wished to guard their trade routes to India. Before the construction of the Suez Canal, ships bound to and from India had to sail south through the Atlantic, rounding what was known as the Cape of Good Hope, before heading north to Asia. The Napoleonic Wars provided the perfect opportunity to gain a foothold there and the first British troops landed in what became the Cape Colony in 1806. Eight years later, the territory was formally ceded to Britain.

Many of the Dutch farmers and merchants living at the Cape did not wish to become part of a British colonial possession and so, over the course of time, made their way north; setting up two independent republics. These were the Orange Free State and the South African Republic; more commonly known as the Transvaal. The Dutch living in these new states were called by the British 'Boers', which means 'farmers'. They preferred to call themselves 'Burghers' or citizens.

As the nineteenth century drew on, there were various developments which made amicable relations between the Dutch republics and the British Cape Colony all but impossible. One notable event was the discovery of gold in the Transvaal. Such treasure was very attractive to the British and in 1880, there was an attempt to annex the Transvaal. This became known as the First Boer War. By 1899, another problem had arisen, which was that the Transvaal was arming itself heavily and had also enlisted the help and advice of German military experts. When the British finally went to war on various pretexts, such as the rights of foreigners living and working within the two Boer republics, most people assumed that there would be a brief struggle, before the tiny nations were decisively crushed by the might of the greatest empire the world had ever known.

The Second Boer War began in October 1899 and, to begin with at least, the Boers managed to carry the war into British territory, causing the army to retreat to various garrison towns such as Mafeking and Ladysmith; which the Boer forces then besieged. All of this was a terrible shock for the British public, who were accustomed to their army beating any opponent. It must be recalled that most of the British army's actions in the late nineteenth century had been against poorly equipped natives, who were no match for well-armed colonial troops. Facing foes who had up-to-date rifles and 155 mm artillery at their disposal was a novel and not altogether pleasing experience for the British army in Africa.

It took four or five months for Britain to transport enough troops and equipment to South Africa to turn the tide of the war in her favour. Field Marshal Lord Roberts was appointed Commander in Chief and adopted an aggressive policy which paid off in a short time. On 13 March 1900, British forces entered Bloemfontein, the capital of the Orange Free State, and by the middle of May, Mafeking had been relieved. On 28

May, the Orange Free State was annexed and a week later, the British captured Pretoria; the capital of the Transvaal. The Boer armies had been comprehensively defeated in the field and by all the usual rules of warfare, the war could be considered to have ended in a decisive victory for Britain. On 29 November 1900, Field Marshal Roberts believed the war to be over and left the country, handing over to his second in command: Lord Kitchener.

The fiercely independent Boers however, were playing by an entirely different set of rules to the British. Having seen their capital cities fall to a foreign invader and their armies swept aside on the field, the Boers decided that the war would need to be prosecuted by other means. The method which they adopted was to launch a ferocious guerrilla war, a series of hit and run attacks on the armed forces occupying their countries.

Central to all guerrilla wars, and crucial to their success, is the attitude of the civilian population. Mao Tse Tung, whose own guerrilla campaign captured for him the most populous nation on earth, said that 'The guerrilla must move among the people as a fish swims in the sea.' In other words, the goodwill of the people is vital to the guerrilla. In the case of the Boer republics, the armed forces of the Transvaal and Orange Free State certainly enjoyed the almost unanimous support of the Dutch settlers. Since most of the men were fighting the British, this meant that the great majority of the civilian population were women and children; the families of the men at war. This presented the Lord Kitchener and his army with a great problem.

In fact, the families of the Boer fighters posed several, closely interwoven problems for the British, all of which were ultimately to be solved in one way. To begin with, it was known that the women and children living in the farmhouses dotted about the land were in the main wholeheartedly in favour of what their men folk were doing. This meant that they observed the movements of British troops and passed on this information to the men in the field. They also fed the soldiers from the produce of their farms. The British, realising that they were, as they saw it, being constantly betrayed to their enemies, began to exact harsh reprisals for any attacks. The actual enemy being so elusive, these reprisals were made against the women and children whose husbands and fathers were at war.

As early as January 1900, before Field Marshal Roberts arrived in South Africa, farmhouses were being burned down by the British forces and those living in them rendered homeless.

Once Roberts had taken charge of the campaign against the Boers, he instituted a systematic policy of the destruction of homes. This included not only individual houses, but also entire towns. From March to June 1900, for instance, Roberts authorised the burning of farms from which snipers had been firing on British troops. Attacks on railways and telegraph lines were causing serious problems for the British and so on 16 June 1900, orders were given that homesteads could be burned and crops and livestock confiscated in a radius of ten miles from any acts of sabotage. This meant that the cutting of a telegraph wire might cause the destruction of farms over an area of 300 or so square miles.

Having embarked upon a course of action which was guaranteed to create refugees, the British army attempted to exploit these homeless people and use them to put pressure on the Boer fighters. In July 1900, Roberts ordered that 2,500 women and children be rounded up and taken by rail to Boer military positions in the Transvaal. They were abandoned there in the open. The aim was to put pressure on the Boers, by showing them how their wives and children would suffer if they continued to fight. This cynical use of families and their treatment as hostages did not have the desired effect. The burning of their farms and enforced homelessness of their families only made the majority of the fighters all the more determined to continue the war.

Some of the actions taken by the British army would today be considered war crimes. In October 1900, for example, Lieutenant-General Sir Archibald Hunter decided that the town of Bothaville in the Orange Free State was a hotbed of guerrilla activity. He ordered his men to burn the town to the ground; sparing only the church, Red Cross centre and several municipal buildings.

By November 1900, the Boer armies in the field had been defeated and Field Marshal Roberts left the country, after declaring the war to be over and handing over command to Lord Kitchener. Kitchener was of course to become famous a few years later for the First World War recruiting poster which bore his portrait. After he had assumed control of the army in South Africa, on 29 November 1900, Kitchener came to the conclusion that if the Boers would not accept their defeat gracefully, but continued with their hit-and-run attacks on his forces, he would have to adopt sterner measures. Not only were individual farmhouses now burned to the ground, but more towns were also obliterated. Soon after Lord Kitchener took over supreme command, the towns of Wolmaransstad, Bethal, Ermelo, Carolina, Reitz, Parys and Lindley were all destroyed by fire. Needless to say, this did nothing to ameliorate the growing refugee crisis.

The military problem for the British was that as soon as they had captured an area from the Boers and moved on to the next part of the country, the Boer guerrillas moved in and reoccupied the land which the British thought that they had seized. In open battle, the Boers could not hope to challenge the enormous forces which the British had now marshalled against them, but with the assistance of the inhabitants of the supposedly conquered districts, the guerrillas were able to prevent the British army exercising any real control over the vast tracts of country in which they were operating.

The establishment of the first concentration camps of the South African War was not part of a coherent and planned policy, but rather an *ad hoc* solution to the growing numbers of refugees created by the deliberate actions of the British forces. In July 1900, a camp was set up near Mafeking for homeless women and children and two months later protective camps were erected at Bloemfontein and Pretoria. These were intended as shelter for the families of Boers who had laid down their arms and surrendered, but they also contained what the British termed 'undesirables'. These were people who were still opposed to the British, whose husbands and fathers were fighting a ferocious guerrilla war, but whose homes had been destroyed. They had nowhere else to go but to these camps.

Having announced that the war had been won, it was a considerable embarrassment for the leaders of the British army to find that their columns were still being ambushed and their communications disrupted by irregular troops who materialised from nowhere and then faded back into the landscape after the attacks. They determined upon a strategy which would, it was thought, bring the war to a final close. The Boer forces were being sustained by the civilian population in the Orange Free State and Transvaal. Very well then, the population would simply be removed and the countryside denuded of any shelter or sustenance for the Boer guerrillas. The aim would be to concentrate the women and children left on the farms into camps which would be guarded by the army. These were, logically enough, called in consequence 'concentration camps'. It was the very same strategy pursued in Cuba by General Weyl six years earlier; a method of warfare that had been widely condemned in England at the time.

The concentration camps were to be one strand of the British strategy for ending the irregular warfare being waged against them. The other was to be the building of thousands of blockhouses, small stone forts, which would be connected by miles of barbed wire. In this way, the vast, open spaces through which the Boers roamed, and which they knew infinitely better than the occupying army, would be subdivided into smaller and more manageable areas which could be systematically swept for guerrillas.

Eventually, 8,000 blockhouses were built; connected by a staggering 4,000 miles of barbed wire fencing. Those living within the areas enclosed in this way were driven from their homes and herded into the new camps. Crops were destroyed and livestock either taken for use by the army or simply killed and left to rot. As Kitchener explained in December 1900, only a few weeks after taking command, 'Every farm is an intelligence agency and a supply depot that it is almost impossible to surround or catch'. Three months later, he enlarged upon his policy, setting out the reasons why it was necessary to herd together the families of the men in the field, Speaking of the women left behind to tend the farms, Kitchener said, 'They give complete intelligence to the Boers of all our movements'. Clearly, this army of spies would need to be moved out of the way if the army were to be successful in crushing the fighters who harried them at every opportunity.

The so-called 'scorched earth' policy which Kitchener adopted was ultimately successful, but at an enormous cost in human life. From January 1901 onwards, this strategy of removing everybody from the land

and destroying any supplies of grain, herds of cattle or other foodstuff from the farms was vigorously pursued until by the autumn of that year 110,000 people, chiefly women and children, were detained and the countryside was neatly divided up into manageable areas surrounded by barbed wire and ringed with stout blockhouses. These zones could then be methodically swept for guerrillas.

Providing adequate food, shelter and medical attention for over 100,000 people would prove a mammoth undertaking for any organisation. Certainly the British army at the turn of the nineteenth century was not equipped for such a task. The first camps had been hastily erected and nobody had thought in detail about the logistics of housing tens of thousands of women and children in makeshift accommodation for months, perhaps years, on end.

It was early in 1901 that the expression 'concentration camp' first entered the English language. In the last chapter, we saw that those interned in the Cuban camps during the 1890s were referred to by the Spanish word recontrentrados. Now, for the first time, the camps themselves were being called, 'concentration camps'. One of the earliest uses of the term is to be found in the records of *Hansard*, which contains *verbatim* accounts of debates in the British parliament. On 5 March 1901, for instance, C.P. Scott, the MP for Leigh, rose to ask the Secretary of State for War a question about the rations provided for the inmates of the camps. He said:

> *I beg to ask the Secretary of State for War if he can now state that the wives and children of Boers in the field are placed on precisely the same rations in the concentration camps as the other women and children, or whether a distinction is still maintained; and, in the latter case, whether he will give instructions that all should be treated alike.*

Mr Broderick, the Secretary for War, brushed off this question by assuring the House of Commons that Lord Kitchener was taking every step possible to ensure that all refugees were being treated humanely. When he was pressed, he simply said that he was leaving Kitchener a free hand and that he would make whatever arrangements he found necessary.

From the very beginning, conditions in the camps were hopelessly inadequate and grew worse as time passed. Things were already grim enough when Emily Hobhouse sailed for the Cape on 7 December 1900, intending to deliver aid. Hobhouse was a well-connected woman and carried an introduction to the British High Commissioner in the Cape: Alfred Milner. With his permission and with the reluctant agreement of Lord Kitchener, Emily Hobhouse was allowed to travel to Bloemfontein, taking with her one railway truck full of supplies for the women and children in the camps.

The concentration camps that Hobhouse visited were much worse than any of the rumours reaching England had suggested. When she arrived, on 24 January 1901, at Bloemfontein, she discovered that accommodation was in tents which were unbearably hot during the day and at night allowed heavy dew to soak those within; clothes were wringing wet in the morning. Two or three families occupied each small tent. Since the average size of the tents was a mere 500 cubic feet, this made living conditions cramped and unhygienic for the ten or twelve people who might be sharing the space. There was no proper sanitation and drinking water was fetched from nearby rivers and drunk without first being boiled. The primitive arrangements for the latrines, no more than trenches dug in the ground, meant that sewage leaked freely from them, this also meant that the water supply was frequently contaminated with raw sewage. Little wonder then that typhoid was endemic.

Typhoid fever was not the only disease to spread like wildfire in the camps. Dysentery, measles, pneumonia and bronchitis were also widespread. Three factors made epidemics of deadly illness almost inevitable. The first was that the majority of residents in the concentration camps were children. This was hardly surprising. For each adult woman, there were generally a number of children. Children are of course more vulnerable to illness than adults and more likely to fall prey to complications. Most of the dead were children under sixteen. The second factor was the lack of soap and water for washing. Soap was a luxury which the army did not feel obliged to supply for those in their camps. The water which was available was often filthy and unsuitable for either drinking or washing. It might be argued that those running the concentration camps had little control over these factors and the resultant deaths. The third reason for the increasingly high mortality rate was however a direct consequence of official policy.

There were two sorts of families in the camps of South Africa. First, there were the wives and children of men who had surrendered to the British and were no longer actively opposing the army. There were also the dependants of men who were still resisting, those still engaged in a bitter struggle with what they regarded as an enemy army of occupation. These two types were known in Afrikaans, for obvious reasons, as *bittereinders* and *hensoppers*. It was felt that the families of the men who were no longer fighting deserved some extra consideration and this was given in the form of increased rations. The rations provided for the inmates of the concentration camps were not lavish and giving more to some meant, inevitably, less for others. In effect, this policy meant that the children of men still on active service did not receive sufficient food to maintain their health and vitality. They were accordingly far more likely to succumb to disease and, having fallen ill, were more prone to complications which could prove fatal.

The first prisoners whom Emily Hobhouse encountered at Bloemfontein had not even been allocated tents. They were therefore forced to sleep in the open; even when it was pouring with rain. So little food was being provided for these women and children, that they were literally starving to death.

After making a thorough nuisance of herself, to the extent that Lord Kitchener referred to her privately as 'That bloody woman', Hobhouse succeeded in having soap added to the list of essential rations for the inmates of the camps. She also managed to arrange for kettles to be distributed, so that drinking water could be boiled. Despite her valiant efforts, the situation for many of those in the concentration camps was to deteriorate dramatically in the course of 1901.

When she returned to England, Emily Hobhouse wrote a report which she delivered to the British government. She called it, *Report of a Visit to the Camps of Women and Children in the Cape and Orange River Colonies.* It was not handed to the government until 1 June 1901, by which time there was increasing unease in many quarters about the stories coming out of South Africa. Try as they might, the Conservative government led by the Marquess of Salisbury was unable to silence the critics and ultimately felt obliged to set up a commission to investigate Hobhouse's claims.

Two weeks after Emily Hobhouse's report was sent to the government, Henry Campbell-Bannerman, Liberal MP and Leader of the Opposition, gave a speech at the Holborn Restaurant in which he coined the phrase which has ever since been associated with the Boer War. On 14 June 1901, he told his audience:

A phrase often used is that 'war is war', but when one comes to ask about it one is told that no war is going on, that it is not war. When is a war not a war? When it is carried on by methods of barbarism in South Africa.

Another point to which Campbell-Bannerman drew attention in his speech was the shockingly high mortality rates in the concentration camps. All this piled pressure on the government and the following month Millicent Fawcett, leader of the National Union of Women's Suffrage Societies, sailed for South Africa, having been asked by Salisbury's government to investigate the camps and to see if there was any truth in the allegations being made by Emily Hobhouse and others.

Before looking at the death rates in the camps, we should perhaps remind ourselves that the late Victorian world was a very different one from our own. Even in a civilised, industrial country like Britain, the death rate was a good deal higher than is now the case. It would be pointless to compare the mortality in the South African camps with that in modern Britain. Instead, we should see the figures in perspective; setting them side by side with the statistics for those who were not living in the camps. The slums of industrial cities in Northern England at the beginning of the twentieth century will give us a good yardstick, as the death rates in those areas were the highest in Britain and regarded by many as scandalous.

In July, August and September of 1901, the death rate in the English city of Newcastle was 25 per 1,000 per year. For Liverpool, it was 23 per 1,000. These figures were among the highest in the whole of Britain and reflected the poor living conditions in slums at that time. The statistics from the South African camps for the same period were almost unbelievable. In August 1901, 2,666 people, most of them children, died in the concentration camps. This worked out at an annual mortality rate of 311 per 1,000. Two months later, in October, 3,205 died in the course of the month; a death rate of 344 per 1,000 per year. In other words, deaths in the camps were running at about fifteen times the level of the worst slums in Britain.

The above figures represent the combined totals for all the camps. There was considerable individual variation, with some camps having far higher death rates than others. At the beginning of August 1901, there were 976 prisoners at the Vereen camp in the Transvaal; of whom fifty died that month. This gives a staggering annual death rate of 582 per 1,000. In other words, if nothing changed, more than half of those in the camp could expect to die of hunger or disease in the course of the following year.

By September 1901, there were thirty-four concentration camps for whites in South Africa, containing around 110,000 people. By the time that peace came in 1902, 26,251 women and children had died in them, as well as 1,676 men; most of them elderly. To understand the significance of these figures, we must bear in mind that the total Boer population of the Transvaal and Orange Free State were only 148,000 Boers in the Transvaal and another 71,000 in the Orange Free State. About a quarter of those held in the camps died, which was roughly 15 per cent of the total Boer population of the two independent republics.

There were separate concentration camps for black people, although their suffering did not excite the same sympathy in Britain as that of the white Boers. Both Emily Hobhouse and Millicent Fawcett appeared to be a good deal more concerned about the plight of the white families than they were with the situation of those in the camps for blacks.

Kitchener had two motives for rounding up the black inhabitants of the Boer republics and placing them too in concentration camps; neither of which was humanitarian. On the one hand, he wished to make quite sure that none of the black servants or farm workers offered aid and comfort to the guerrillas. Secondly, the British army needed a large number of labourers to help with building the blockhouses, laying the barbed wire and so on. It seemed to Lord Kitchener only logical to impress black men for labour. This explains why during the sweeps in which both blacks and whites were captured, native villages as well as farms were targeted by the troops. It was not only Boer farmhouses which were burned, African kraals were treated in the same way.

By July 1901, some 38,000 blacks were being held in special camps; over 30,000 of them being women and children. Thousands of black men were taken into the service of the army, while others were sent to work in the gold mines. The white camps were provided with tents, however leaky and draughty these might have been. Nothing of the sort was thought necessary for the blacks, who were expected to build their own dwellings.

As in the white camps, the mortality rate rose throughout 1901. Roughly the same number of black people as white were being held in concentration camps by the end of the war in 1902. In December 1901, 2,831 of these prisoners died, giving an annual death rate of 372 per 1,000. This was a little higher than the mortality rate for the white camps, which peaked in October 1901 at 344 per 1,000. Nevertheless, 14,154 black people are recorded as having died in the camps in total; fewer than in the white camps.

By modern standards, the actions of the British army in the Boer War were brutal in the extreme. We do not tend to look kindly these days on armies that deliberately burn civilians' homes and then lock them in concentration camps, where they die of hunger and disease. We might term such tactics 'ethnic cleansing'. Even bearing in mind the difference in perception over the last 115 years or so, surely most people in Britain would have been shocked and horrified to hear about these actions? The fact is, there was very little sympathy for the Boers and most people in Britain felt that they were getting what they deserved.

The early reverses suffered by the British army in South Africa came as a dreadful shock to many people. The British had become accustomed over the years to winning wars swiftly and putting upstart countries in their place without too much trouble. The sieges that the Boer forces were able to mount against the Cape towns of Mafeking and Ladysmith were something of a novelty. Imagine British forces being cooped up and kept at bay by a handful of foreigners! When news came of the relief of Mafeking, there was wild rejoicing across the whole of Britain. There were also riots, in which the homes of those felt to be 'pro-Boer' were attacked and the windows smashed. Anybody siding with the enemy was felt to be unpatriotic.

Later on, when the Boers resorted to guerrilla warfare, this too infuriated many people in Britain. Such methods of warfare were seen as sneaky and underhand. Honest soldiers faced each other squarely on the battlefield; there was none of these hit and run attacks and sabotage by night. Both the army in the field and the civilians and politicians at home believed that by carrying on in this way, the Boers had somehow put themselves beyond the pale and deserved everything they got.

That this was the official view may be seen by looking at what the army commanders in South Africa said at the time. By the summer of 1900, when questions were already being asked about the policy of burning the homes of civilians, Lord Roberts had defended the use of such tactics as the only means at his disposal to tackle guerrilla fighters. Much as he regretted it, he was forced to rely upon, 'Those exceptional methods which civilised nations have found it obligatory to use under like circumstances'.

It might be worth mentioning at this point that the Boers themselves were not above striking at civilians if it seemed to suit their purposes. It might seem to us barbaric to destroy the homes of non-combatants in the way that Roberts and Kitchener were doing, but during the sieges of cities such as Kimberly, the Boers surrounded cities with heavy artillery and shelled them indiscriminately. The guns which they had acquired from the Germans in the years before the outbreak of war were thus used to hurl high explosives not at an enemy army, but into the heart of civilian areas. Even worse was the attempt to spread highly infectious and lethal diseases.

When, early in 1900, Lord Roberts had captured Bloemfontein, capital of the Orange Free State, he believed that the war was within measurable distance of its end. In fact, the occupation by the British army of Bloemfontein signalled the first large-scale guerilla action of the Boer war. On 31 March 1900, 2,000 men under the command of the Boer General Christiaan de Wet advanced to Sanna's Post, some twenty miles from Bloemfontein. The British army had a small garrison there; centred around the waterworks which served the city. The attack on Sanna's Post was a brilliant success for the Boers. By the time that the fighting was over, the British had lost 155 men and the Boers only three.

It was the aftermath of the attack which captured the waterworks, which was deadly. There had already been cases of cholera among the British troops in Bloemfontein. When the supply of clean water was cut off, the isolated cases turned into an epidemic which claimed the lives of over 2,000 British soldiers.

Actions of this sort, the shelling of civilian districts and precipitation of epidemics of disease, took place before the widespread use of concentration camps. They created anger and hostility against the Boers; both in the British army in the field and also the public back in Britain itself. The Boers, it was widely felt, had placed themselves beyond the pale by using such tactics and the British army had been forced to counter these unconventional acts of war by whatever means it had at its disposal.

A recurring theme in this book is the surprising way in which aspects of Nazi Germany's treatment of its supposed enemies has been foreshadowed in the actions of the British; in some cases thirty or forty years earlier. A case in point is the way in which the Boers were represented and described. One of the most important points to note when persecuting or mistreating some opponent of your government is to try and portray these enemies as being less than human. The Nazis were of course experts at this strategy. They used expressions such as 'vermin' when talking of the Jews and did their best to persuade their citizens that Jews were an inferior and dangerous form of humanity; closer to animals than real humans.

In 1901, at the height of the Boer War, a book was published in England, called, *On Yeoman Service; Being the Diary of the Wife of an Imperial Yeomanry Officer, During the Boer War.* The author was Lady Maud Rolleston and her views and opinions of the Boers whom she encountered during the war are enough to cause modern readers to draw in their breath rather sharply. She wrote:

> *I can only say that I much disliked their aspect... their countenances are singularly deficient in nobility: the eyes are generally small and dark, and very close together, the nose is short and insignificant, the drooping moustache, which usually conceals the upper lip, shows the lower one to be large and sensual... the face is, to my thinking, nearly always animal... the glance is shifty, and reminds me irresistibly of a visit to the zoological gardens at home.*

Lady Rolleston was not alone in the unfavourable impression which the Boers made upon her. Popular magazines covering the war in South Africa, publications such as *Under the Union Jack* and *Pearson's War Pictures*, referred to the Boers in animal terms as, 'herds', 'flocks' 'swarms and 'droves'. A colonel of the Connaught Rangers wrote that he thought the Boers, 'reptilian' in appearance and found them, 'quite hideous to look on'.

Hand-in-hand with the brutish appearance of the Boers, soldiers and civilians, went primitive habits and unclean behaviour. It might be mentioned here that some Nazis involved with running concentration camps blamed the unhygienic ways of the prisoners for the outbreaks of disease which killed so many of them. By this reading of the situation, those who died of typhoid at Belsen were really the authors of their own misfortune! If only they had washed their hands more frequently, then they would not have died like flies. Almost unbelievably, this is precisely the explanation advanced in 1901 for the shockingly high mortality rates in the camps of South Africa.

John Buchan, the author of *The Thirty Nine Steps*, was the private secretary of Alfred Milner, who, during the Boer War, was Governor of the Cape Colony. Buchan blamed the conditions in the concentration camps, which he admitted were, 'distressing', on the fact that the prisoners were, 'mentally and bodily underbred'. They were 'a class of people who have somehow missed civilisation'. At the same time that John Buchan was expressing such views, a Dr John Welenski, writing in the November 1901 edition of the *British Medical Journal*, was attributing the thousands of deaths in the camps to the 'fecklessness, ignorance and dirtiness' of the Boer mothers whose children were dying like flies. Even the Prime Minister, Lord Salisbury, had something to say on the subject. He told a clergyman, anxious about the terrible conditions in the concentration camps that there could not fail to be 'a great mortality; particularly among a people so dirty as the Boers'.

This then was the British conclusion; the horrific death rate in the camps which they had set up was really the fault of the victims themselves! It might seem to us today all but incredible that even the most callous and hardened person could pass such a judgement, but this was the standard attitude of those in Britain who were challenged about what, even then, looked very much like an act of mass murder. Lord Kitchener held the strongest of such views, giving it as his own opinion that the deaths of tens of thousands of children was the direct consequence of what he called 'the criminal neglect of the mothers'. Kitchener thought that in some cases, the mothers 'ought to be tried for manslaughter'.

At first, the South African concentration camps were under the direct control of the military, but as this changed, so conditions improved and the death toll dropped. There can be no doubt that the the activities of people like Emily Hobhouse and Millicent Fawcett helped to draw attention in Britain to the dreadful situation, which was further publicised by the Liberal leader; Henry Campbell-Bannerman. Throughout most of 1901, when the mortality rate was at its highest, the civil authorities were nominally in charge of the camps, although in practice they were being administered by the army. It was not until November 1901 that active control of the concentration camps was taken out of the hands of the military and the number of monthly deaths began to fall dramatically. In October 1901, the month before the civil authorities assumed real control, there were 3,205 deaths. By March 1902, this had dropped to 412 and two months later, only 196 people died in the space of a month. It appeared that the appalling number of deaths from hunger and disease had been a direct consequence of army policy towards their prisoners.

The evidence at which we have so far looked seems pretty damning. There can be no doubt that the British army conducted a campaign using methods which would today be classed as war crimes. They burned homes, sometimes even entire towns, and then drove those whom they had rendered homeless into concentration camps, where the conditions were so awful that they died at an astonishingly high rate. As soon as the control of these camps was wrested from the military, the death rate fell, until it was barely a twentieth of what it had been when the army was in charge. All of this is indisputable, but there is, nevertheless, something to be said in defence of Lord Kitchener and his 'methods of barbarism'.

The Boer War is sometimes described as the first 'modern' war fought by the British. Previous wars had been fought with nineteenth-century technology and weapons; frequently against pitifully armed foes such as African tribesmen brandishing spears. This was a war against a well-armed enemy, which was using up-to-date rifles and heavy artillery. Indeed, the Mausers used by the Boers were in many ways superior to the Lee-Metford and Lee-Enfield rifles issued to the British troops. Combine this with the fact that for the first time in fifty years or so, British soldiers in the field found themselves under bombardment by artillery and you begin to understand what a shocking experience this particular colonial war proved to the British, right from the beginning.

Not only were there new weapons to contend with, hitherto unknown tactics too were employed. Guerrilla warfare had been known in the past, but this was the first time that the British army had encountered well-armed and determined guerrillas. It was all rather shocking and it comes perhaps as no surprise that it took the British generals some time to work out an effective response to the threats that they were facing. Among the methods chosen to counter the threats faced by the men in the field was of course the policy of concentrating the population in special camps.

In fairness to the army, it should be mentioned that they not only had little idea of the immense task which they were undertaking, but that they did not have the resources to support any large number of civilians in reasonable conditions. The reason for this was that they themselves were not really coping very well during this war. Quite apart from the fact that they were facing a ferocious battle for every inch of territory that they seized, the troops were trying to survive in an environment quite unlike the British Isles. Many of these men were recent conscripts and had no idea at all of how to stay healthy and safe in South Africa, rather than the East End of London. The deaths from disease among the prisoners held in the camps was indeed very high, but the army also suffered greatly from cholera and typhoid. Around 22,000 British soldiers died during the course of the Boer War, but only a minority fell victim to Boer bullets and artillery. Almost two thirds of these deaths, 13,000, were due to illness.

In short, the army itself was struggling to cope for much of the time during the Boer War. If they could not prevent over 10,000 of their own men dying from faecal-oral infections; what hope for the many thousands of women and children being held captive by those same soldiers? It is possible to argue that those in the camps were really only being expected to endure the same hazards, risks and hardships as the soldiers whose job it was to guard them. The difference was of course that the British soldiers had all volunteered; they were in this position through their own choice. The same could not be said of the 110,000 Boers and 38,000 Africans who were being detained in concentration camps between 1900 and 1902.

What then is the final verdict on Lord Kitchener's camps? Did they really constitute, as some Afrikaaner historians maintain, a form of genocide? It is of course notoriously difficult, and some would say fruitless, to judge the past by the standards of the present. The best that we can perhaps say is that if any country's army behaved today as Lord Kitchener's did in the opening years of the last century, then we would have no doubt that a series of war crimes were being committed. Let us recall one final time the casualty toll of the camps. Altogether, 27,927 Boers and 14,154 Africans died in the concentration camps; a total of 42,081 people, the great majority of whom were children under the age of sixteen. By any standards, not just those of today but also those of a century or more ago this was shocking in the extreme.

We might end this examination of the first concentration camp system to be established in the twentieth century by looking once more at the definition of genocide which was adopted by the United Nations in 1948. Genocide was defined as, 'any of the following acts committed with the intent to destroy, in whole or in part, a national, ethnic, racial or religious group, as such'. The Convention on Genocide went on to list various obvious means of committing genocide by slaughtering members of ethnic or religious minorities. Also included was 'Deliberately inflicting on the group conditions of life calculated to bring about its physical destruction in whole or part'. Judged by this, there can be little doubt that the British treatment of both Boers and Africans during the South African War did indeed amount to genocide.

Chapter Three

1914-1918
England, Scotland and Wales: Three Different
Kinds of Concentration Camps of the
First World War

1. Frongoch: The Republican University

On 21 March 1933 the Chief of Police in the German city of Munich, one Heinrich Himmler, released a statement to the press in which he announced the opening of the first concentration camp in the country. Himmler's problem was that scattered throughout the Bavarian prison system were hundreds of political opponents of the government; men who were regarded by the National Socialists as representing a danger to the security of the state. It was difficult to keep track of these people when they were held in so many different places, therefore Himmler wished to see them 'concentrated' together in one location. The new camp had been established in and around a disused factory near the town of Dachau; ten miles North West of Munich.

Seventeen years before the opening of Dachau, there was an eerie foreshadowing of Himmler's prototypical concentration camp. In precisely the same way as in 1930s Germany, the prisons of a European country had become clogged up with political cases; hundreds of men being held without charge, who were believed to pose a threat to the nation's stability. Just as with Dachau, the idea was hit upon to concentrate these political prisoners in a special camp, situated in an out of the way location. Like Dachau, the camp was centred around a derelict factory; only this camp, rather than being in Bavaria, was to be found in the heart of the Welsh countryside.

We should pause for a moment and consider that concentration camps of this sort, where political prisoners are being held, are rather different from those at which we have so far been looking. In Cuba and South Africa, the aim was .to 'concentrate' entire populations, who might be opposed to those ruling the country, in one place; thus depriving guerrilla fighters of their support base. Depopulating an area of open country makes it far easier to track down and eliminate any irregular forces who might be operating in the area. In the case both of Dachau and also Frongoch, the Welsh concentration camp, the idea was to avoid cluttering up one's prison system with too many political cases. It must also be remembered that the expression 'concentration camp' had not yet acquired the hideous overtones of genocide and mass murder. British newspapers referred openly during the First World War to concentration camps being operated in the United Kingdom.

In 1889, an Englishman called Edward Nicholls purchased some land in Merionethshire, North Wales, with the aim of building a distillery near the hamlet of Frongoch. The site was chosen because of the purity of the Tryweryn river which ran through the area and the Welsh Whiskey Distillery Ltd operated there until 1900. Substantial stone buildings were erected and the enterprise provided employment to local men and women. It was not however a commercial success and in 1900 the undertaking was acquired by William Owen of the White Lion Hotel in Bala. He paid £5,000 for the business and launched a new brand of whiskey produced at Frongoch, which he named 'Royal Welsh Whisky'.

By 1910, William Owen too had found that the manufacture of Welsh whisky was not a profitable enterprise and so the distillery closed. For the next four years, the buildings at Frongoch were abandoned and became semi-derelict.

When war broke out in 1914, the owner of the abandoned distillery saw an opportunity to recoup some of the money lost in the abortive whisky business. He leased the factory and surrounding land to the British government for use as a prisoner of war camp. During 1915 and 1916, Frongoch camp contained German prisoners, who were discouraged from escaping by the fact that they were being held in an exceedingly remote area.

On Monday, 24 April 1916, which happened to be Easter Monday that year, a body of Irish volunteers seized various buildings in the centre of Dublin. These included the General Post Office. In the following days, the British army suppressed what later became known as the Easter Rising with great ferocity; using heavy artillery to shell the city. Within less than a week, it was all over and the majority of the 1,200 or so men and handful of women who had taken part in the insurrection, along with many others who just happened to be on the streets at the wrong time, were prisoners of the army.

Coming, as it did, at the height of the war, this attempt at revolution was seen by most people in both Britain and Ireland as an act of treachery. The prisoners were jeered and spat at by the citizens of Dublin when they were marched through the streets and the soldiers guarding them were forced to protect their charges from lynch mobs of angry Irishmen. In the aftermath of the Rising, a number of the leaders were executed by firing squads after summary courts martial and the remainder deported to the British mainland. Once there, these men, none of whom had been charged with any offence, were distributed throughout the prison system. They were held in both civilian prisons such as Glasgow, Perth and Reading, and also in military detention centres such as that at Stafford in the Midlands.

During the Easter Rising and in the days following the defeat of the Irish bid for independence, the British army seized thousands of men and kept them prisoner without charge. Some were released, but over 2,500 were shipped across the Irish Sea and placed in English and Scottish prisons while the government considered what to do with them. For a month, the prisons of Britain were crowded with men who had been charged with nothing, many of whom were almost certainly guilty of nothing; having been unlucky enough to have lived or worked near districts where the rebels were fighting. To release them was unthinkable, but their continued detention, scattered as they were throughout the whole country, meant that it was hard to keep track of them all. Far better, thought ministers in London, if they could all be concentrated together in one spot. At least then, the authorities would know where they were and what they were up to.

Throughout May 1916, the German prisoners of war at Frongoch Camp were dispersed to other locations, until by the end of the month, the camp was empty. Then, on 9 June, Irish prisoners began arriving there. At its peak, Frongach contained over 2,000 prisoners, or 'detainees' as they were more correctly known. After all, they had not been charged with, let alone convicted of, anything at all. Their legal position was vague. They themselves claimed to be prisoners of war, but the British rejected this idea, only to accept it later when it suited their purposes. The men at Frongoch were served with notices stating that they were being interned under the Defence of the Realm Regulations. The reason given was that they had been members of organisations called either the Irish Volunteers or the Citizen Army; organisations which had promoted armed insurrection against His Majesty King George V.

Frongoch was soon renamed by the inmates as Francach; a word which literally means a Frenchman, but is used colloquially in Gaelic to refer to a rat. The camp was divided in two. The original buildings of the distillery formed South Camp, while North Camp consisted of wooden huts. Both camps were surrounded by barbed wire and guarded by soldiers. From the start, there was friction between those who had been legitimately arrested after taking part in armed action in Dublin over Easter Week and innocent passers-by who had simply been caught in the military sweeps which followed the Rising. According to one of the more well-known detainees, Michael Collins, about a quarter of the inmates of the North Camp had not been involved in any way with the abortive revolution. They not unnaturally felt aggrieved by their position.

None of those brought to Frongoch had the slightest idea how long they would be held in the newly established concentration camp, nor what was likely to be their eventual fate. There were rumours that there might be further courts martial and perhaps even more executions. In the event, the worst thing that happened was that some high-ranking leaders of the Rising were tried and sent to civilian prisons to serve their sentences. Some of the leaders of the revolt who had not been shot were already serving sentences of life imprisonment in English prisons. It was an alarming prospect for the men at Frongoch, that they too might end up being imprisoned for life in an English gaol.

The authorities were in no hurry to decide anything about the final disposition of these men and so as the summer drew on, they languished in the camp. It was not even possible for them to be certain about their status. Attempts were made in the House of Commons to establish the position of the men at Frongoch, but the government remained strangely coy about them.

On 6 July 1916, a month or so after the prisoners had arrived at Frongoch, Major Newman, the Member of Parliament for Enfield, asked 'Are those who fought for the Republic of Ireland now recognised as prisoners of war?' The Speaker responded coldly 'That question does not arise. It is only put to irritate.' Before the year was out though, fifteen of the men being held at Frongoch would be facing a military court, charged with offences against the discipline of prisoners of war.

Despite the short and chilly responses given in the House of Commons by government spokesmen, when asked about the Frongoch camp, questions continued throughout the time of the camp's existence. These questions were really designed to draw the attention of the public to the fact that citizens of the United Kingdom were being held without trial in a concentration camp. On 4 July, for example, Mr Alfred Byrne, a Dublin MP, asked the Under-Secretary for War if it would be possible for prisoners at Frongoch to receive visits on Sundays. On being told that there were not enough staff at the camp to allow for this, another MP, Edward Graham, chipped and told the House that he was very disturbed at the isolation in which the prisoners at Frongoch were being held. He pointed out that it took six hours to reach the camp from London, by railway, and that when MPs visited prisoners there; they were allowed only a quarter of an hour with those they had come to see.

What was it really like in the camp? The best way to get an idea of what conditions were like at Frongoch Concentration Camp, is to listen to the accounts of those who were detained there. One of the most famous prisoners held in the camp was Michael Collins, who had played an active role in the Easter Rising. When Ireland had gained independence, Collins became both Minister of Finance and Director of Intelligence; virtually running the first republican government before he was assassinated during the civil war which followed. In early July 1916 Michael Collins, who was being held at the military detention barracks in Stafford, was transferred to the camp at Frongoch.

When Collins arrived at Frongoch, there had been rain for several days and the entire camp was a mass of slippery mud. He was housed in one of the wooden huts of the North Camp, which were more comfortable than the buildings which made up the old distillery. It didn't take him long to discover that a lot of the men being held at the concentration camp were guilty of nothing more than having been in Dublin during the Easter Rising. He wrote to a friend:

> ... by my own count, at least a quarter of the men in the North camp know very little about the Rising. One man, a former labourer of my acquaintance, said that he was just forced off the street in a round-up. His only crime appears to be that he was walking the streets.

As a senior member of the volunteers who took part in the Rising, Michael Collins found himself placed in charge of one of the huts. The overall head of the prisoners was a man called O'Reilly, who had been Vice-Commandant of the Dublin Brigade. This man tried to force the British to acknowledge the men being held at Frongoch as prisoners of war and to be accorded the treatment to which they would then be entitled under the Geneva Convention. The army officer in charge of the camp ignored all such requests.

It has to be said that for a concentration camp, conditions at Frongoch were not too bad. There was adequate food, the prisoners were allowed to organise themselves and, so long as there was no trouble, the soldiers guarding them left them largely to their own devices. It was this which led to the camp being later referred to as the Republican University. Those who had taken part in the Rising analysed the reasons for its failure and arranged discussion groups about various topics. Some studied Gaelic, others politics. The commandant of the camp, Colonel Heygate-Lambert, made no effort to interfere with what the prisoners did, always providing that Frongoch ran smoothly.

Over the summer, the numbers held at the concentration camp fell, as the results of the work of a body set up in London and called the

Advisory Committee on the Internment of Rebels. Prisoners were taken to London in batches to be screened by this committee. Their aim was twofold. First, they wished to see if it might be possible to court-martial any of the men being held. Secondly, it was known by the authorities, as well as the prisoners themselves, that many completely innocent people were being detained. The Advisory Committee tried to winnow out these men and see that they were released and sent home to Ireland. By the end of August, the 2,000 prisoners had fallen to about 650. Almost all the others had been quietly sent home.

The truth of the matter was that the camp at Frongoch was something of an embarrassment to the government. It was one thing to hold Germans in such camps, but these men were citizens of the United Kingdom and had not even been charged, let alone convicted, with any offence. Their continued detention was doing the reputation of the English government no good in Ireland, or anywhere else for that matter. Here were citizens who were denied any recourse to the courts and were unable to mount any legal challenge to their continued imprisonment. The wholesale shooting of the leaders of the Easter Rising had created a good deal of sympathy for the rebels's cause in Ireland itself; arresting thousands of men, many of them quite blameless, was also helping to create martyrs.

Attempts were constantly being made by Irish Members of Parliament to involve other countries in their complaints. On 7 December, Alfred Byrne asked the Home Secretary, whether, 'it is proposed to allow representatives of the American Embassy to visit Frongoch Camp?' This was hugely embarrassing to the government as they were assiduously courting the Americans, with a view to persuading them to enter the war on Britain's side.

Now that the population of the camp had dropped by two thirds, there was room for all the prisoners in the more comfortable North Camp. The South Camp, the old buildings of the former distillery, were used as a punishment block. For instance at one point, the military administration of the camp ordered the prisoners to start emptying the rubbish bins around the soldiers' barracks. Those who refused to have anything to do with this menial and unpaid work were promptly transferred to the cold and draughty accommodation of the disused factory. An even greater cause of contention was the attempt to get the prisoners to clean the soldiers' latrines; a task which every single prisoner refused to undertake. At one point, over a hundred prisoners who would not clean the latrines were confined to the unpleasant conditions of the South Camp.

In October, the inmates of Frongoch organised a sports day. This was mentioned during a debate in parliament as evidence that things could not be too bad for the prisoners. Just imagine, a concentration camp where those held are allowed to arrange their own sports! One MP suggested that the complaints about food at the camp should not be taken too seriously if the 100-yard race could be won by a prisoner in a little under eleven seconds. This irritated Michael Collins, who pointed out that he and the other men were heavily dependent on food parcels and that if it were not for these, then their physical condition would have been pretty poor. These athletic contests were held in October 1916, but in the background there were more sinister developments; plans were afoot which could have jeopardised the very lives of the men in Frongoch.

On 2 March 1916, the Military Service Act came into force in Britain. Until then, the British army had relied upon volunteers; as had been the case throughout the whole of the country's history. In March 1916 though, single men aged between 18 and 41 years of age no longer had any choice in the matter. They were to be conscripted into the forces against their will. In May, another act broadened the scope of those being conscripted to include married men, as well as bachelors. The Military Service Act covered only men living on the British mainland; England, Scotland and Wales. It did not apply to Ireland. However, Irishmen living in Britain *would* be liable for conscription.

Some time over the summer of 1916, somebody in Whitehall came up with the idea of dealing with the problem of the hundreds of men being held in the Frongoch camp by conscripting them into the army. It was a brilliant scheme. After all, although Irish, all these men were certainly now resident in Britain and therefore theoretically eligible to be drafted into the armed forces. The only difficulty in implementing this plan was that the men at Frongoch somehow got wind of it. Michael Collins reacted angrily and came up with a perfect riposte. From the end of October onwards, he and the other hut leaders ordered that nobody was to answer to his name when addressed by soldiers, or acknowledge his identity in any way to the military authorities of the camp. This would, he thought, prevent any call-up papers being served on prisoners.

It has to be said that the idea of conscripting these men into the army was a peculiarly vindictive one. Once enlisted, they would have a choice. On the one hand, they could refuse to obey orders, when once they had been shipped across to the Western Front in France; in which case they would face court martial and execution. Alternatively, they could stay on the front line and face the likelihood of being killed by the Germans. In either case, they would cease to be a vexatious problem for the British government.

Matters came to a head on 2 November 1916. As a trial run, the army had taken from the camp a man whom they claimed was called Michael Murphy. There was some dispute about the situation; whether Murphy was being called up or if it was being claimed that he was in fact a deserter from the army. Whatever the situation, the army took the wrong man from the camp. When the mistake was discovered, Colonel Heygate-Lambert decided to hold a roll call at Frongoch; the first time that this had been done. On 2 November, he assembled the men and his adjutant called out names, expecting the prisoners to answer and thus identify themselves. Not one did so. This was partly because Michael Murphy, the man wanted by the military, was still in the camp and nobody wished to see him identified. Five days later, on 7 November, another roll call was held, with the same result. Following this, the fifteen hut leaders were charged with a military offence concerning, 'maintaining discipline among prisoners of war'. It had apparently finally been decided that this was the status of the men at Frongoch. They were, after much hedging, admitted to be prisoners of war.

There can be little doubt that the Camp Commandant handled the confrontation very badly. After the abortive roll calls, some of the prisoners went on hunger strike. Another had a nervous breakdown, brought on by his fear of being sent to France as a soldier. After five months in captivity, a number of other men were suffering the consequences of imprisonment and the general health of many was not good. It was now that Colonel Heygate-Lambert played another card. He ruled that the camp doctor, a man called Peters, was not to treat any of the inmates for any condition, until they had correctly identified themselves to him. This meant that none of the men were to receive medical treatment from then on.

Caught between the demands of his conscience and the orders of the Camp Commandant, Dr Peters was in an unenviable position. Some men were on hunger strike and in urgent need of care and attention, but he was forbidden to tend to them until they answered to their names. Dr Peters had already had a run-in with the Camp Commandant about the quality of the food being provided. One consignment of meat was in such an advanced state of decomposition, that the very smell of it made soldiers retch. Nevertheless, Colonel Heygate-Lambert insisted that it be washed with vinegar to remove the smell and then served to the prisoners. The doctor examined this meat for himself and ruled that it was unfit for human consumption.

After various other problems and finding that he was unable to adhere both to his code of ethics and the requirements of the job, Dr Peters wrote out his resignation, but was asked by the Home Office to stay on until some matters had been attended to. He became so distressed about matters that he vanished one day and was later found floating face down in the Tryweryn river, which flowed past the camp. An inquest held in Merioneth found that Dr Peters had committed suicide.

Shortly after the fifteen men were charged and told that they would stand trial before a military court for their refusal to answer to their names, Michael Collins managed to smuggle out an account of the situation in Frongoch. This was passed to a newspaper in Ireland and on 11 November the *Cork Free Press* published details of what was going on at the camp. The story was picked up by the *Manchester Guardian*, who found that legally, reporters were entitled to be present at the trial of the fifteen prisoners. This was the last thing that the government wanted and orders were issued that journalists were to be excluded from the proceedings; an act which would have been quite illegal.

On Saturday 25 November 1916, a military court was convened at Frongoch camp under the authority of a Royal Warrant of 3 August 1914. This allowed the army to impose discipline upon prisoners of war; although its legality when used against the citizens of this country was open to question. The wording of the warrant, which was for, 'the Maintenance of Discipline among Prisoners of War', was as follows:

Whereas We deem it expedient to make regulations for the custody of and maintenance of discipline among prisoners of war interned in the United Kingdom or elsewhere; Our Will and Pleasure is that the custody of and maintenance of discipline among prisoners of war interned in the United Kingdom and elsewhere shall be governed by the laws and customs of war and the regulations attached to this Our Warrant, which regulations shall be the sole authority on the matters therein treated of...

The charges against the prisoners at Frongoch were based upon the regulations cited in the Royal Warrant, namely that:

... any such charge or charges as may be preferred against them for any offence which, if committed in England, would be triable before a Civil Court of Criminal Jurisdiction or for any offence the commission of which shall be held prejudicial to the safety of or well-being of His Majesty's Dominions, armed forces or subjects or to the safe custody, control or well-being of any prisoner of war.

Major E.E. Husey of the Cheshire Regiment was President of the court and the other members were Captain F. Fanning Evans and Captain C.C. Doran. Present as Judge-Advocate was Lieutenant Colonel Ivor Bowen.

The court assembled at a building inside Frongoch Camp and this at once caused a problem. Appendix C of the Royal Warrant under which the trial was being held, specifically stated that, 'all the proceedings shall be in open court and in the presence of the accused'. This was quite unambiguous and a reporter from the *Manchester Guardian* and a journalist from another newspaper arrived in Wales to cover the proceedings. They were stopped at the gates of the camp by armed soldiers, who told them that they would only be admitted if they had a pass from the Commandant, Colonel Heygate-Lambert. He refused permission for anybody to enter the camp without permission from the Home Office. It is entirely possible that the colonel was acting on instructions from the government in taking this stance and it was hoped to avoid any publicity for the trial by this means. If so, the strategy backfired.

George Duffy, the defence counsel for the accused men, drew the court's attention to what was happening and asserted, quite correctly, that unless the trial was held in public, then the court would have no legal standing. The Judge-Advocate agreed with this point and advised the President that the press must be admitted. A sergeant was despatched to the Commandant's office to instruct him to let the reporters in. He refused, saying that he had orders from the Home Office. None of this was making a very good impression on the two journalists, who were preparing to write an account of how prisoners held at Frongoch were being denied a fair and open trial. The *impasse* was resolved by the court removing itself to a building which lay outside the barbed wire fence of the camp itself.

The same charge was faced by all fifteen of the men; namely that after being warned by the Commandant, they failed to answer their names during a roll call. None of those being tried for this offence denied that they had failed to answer to their names, but gave as their defence that they suspected that the roll call, the first held in the camp, was intended to identify men who might be called up for military service. Colonel Heygate-Lambert did not come out very well as the evidence was given. Even the soldiers serving under him testified that he had said and done some exceedingly callous things. Sergeant-Major Newstead testified that the Commandant had said to the prisoners that if he had nothing but dead bodies in the camp, he would have discipline.

There was no doubt that, technically at least, the accused men were guilty of the offence with which they were charged. George Duffy, for the defence, challenged the validity of the trial on various grounds; none of which were accepted by the court. The chief point made on behalf of the defence was that none of the actions of which the fifteen men were accused were illegal under either statute or common law. In short, they had not really committed an offence at all. The idea that laws could be passed in this way, merely by the King's signing a warrant set a dangerous precedent. Parliament had been completely bypassed. Nevertheless, the court refused to accept such arguments and that being so, the case was proved.

The climax of the trial was bathetic in the extreme. The men were all convicted of the charge and it remained only to decide on their punishment. This was solemnly declared to be a month's imprisonment. Since they were already prisoners, it is debatable how much this penalty affected them.

The staff of the *Manchester Guardian* revenged themselves on Colonel Heygate-Lambert for his trying to prevent them from reporting the trial by running several articles which drew attention to Frongoch; the last thing the government wished to see. Throughout late November and the first half of December, more and more questions were being asked in parliament about the conditions at Frongoch and the ultimate fate of the men held there. On 4 December 1916, for instance, questioning from Irish MPs forced the government to admit that efforts had indeed been made to draft some of the prisoners at Frongoch into the army.

By the middle of December, there could be nobody in the British government who did not simply wish to be rid of the men being detained at the camp in Wales. Other political developments were at work; things that had nothing to do with the Irish prisoners and their circumstances as such, but would ultimately bring about a neat and satisfactory resolution of the awkward situation which the British had inadvertently created for themselves. On 7 December 1916, Herbert Asquith, the Prime Minister, was replaced by David Lloyd George. Asquith was a somewhat stuffy and inflexible politician, who had a reputation for standing fast and refusing to compromise. Having already, as he saw it, faced down the suffragettes in the years before the outbreak of war in 1914, he evidently felt that the same strategy might work against the Irish nationalists. This was a disastrous miscalculation and as soon as Asquith was safely out of the saddle, Lloyd George lost no time in reaching a compromise about Frongoch Camp. Perhaps compromise is the wrong way of stating the case; it was more a complete capitulation.

On 21 December 1916, the Secretary of State for Ireland announced that the camp at Frongoch was to be dismantled and all prisoners to be released without charge and sent back to Ireland as free men. The following evening, the camp adjutant at Frongoch, presumably the Commandant himself could not bring himself to admit publicly that his rule was being ignominiously ended, announced to the assembled prisoners that they were all to be released. Astonishingly, most were to be set free that very night. Those who lived in the north, south and west of Ireland would be taken from the camp at once and put on ships bound for Ireland. It was not to be expected that after the history of bitter confrontation which had marked relations in Frongoch between the Irish prisoners and those guarding them, things should now have gone smoothly.

The adjutant asked for the names, addresses and home railway stations of the first few batches of prisoners to be freed and at once, there was an objection from Michael Collins. How did they know, he asked, that this was not some new trap and a way for the army to acquire the information about the identity of the men being held at Frongoch which they had been seeking in vain for the last two months? A tense standoff was averted when the adjutant suggested that the men compile the lists themselves. An hour later, lorries entered the camp and the first group of prisoners was loaded onto them and driven to the port at Holyhead on the Isle of Anglesey. There, they were put on board the overnight ferry to Ireland.

The following day, more prisoners were taken from Frongoch and sent home. According to one, when they changed trains at Chester, the men amused themselves by marching along the platform singing *Deutschland uber Alles*. To the very last, they were determined to be an irritation to the English authorities. The last of the detainees were freed from the camp on the night of Christmas Eve. Michael Collins was one of these; arriving in Dublin early on the morning of Christmas Day.

Thus ended Britain's first experiment with the detention of political prisoners. It had been a largely unedifying spectacle and few in government had any wish to repeat it. The idea of holding one's own citizens in concentration camps in this way had not proved a success and although this method of combating a domestic insurgency was to be used again from time to time over the next sixty years, it was never to become widespread or popular. The same could not be said for locking up foreigners and members of ethnic minorities. Here, the sensibilities of the British were not so easily offended and it was to be many years before rounding up people of particular religions or nationalities was to become seen as unacceptable. Indeed, during the First World War, thousands of foreigners were kept behind barbed wire for no other reason than that they had been born abroad. This kind of thing began soon after the outbreak of war in the summer of 1914.

2. The Concentration Camps for 'Aliens'

On 9 November 1938, mobs in Germany attacked shops and other premises owned by Jews. In a number of cities, synagogues were also burned. The response of the authorities was not to punish the perpetrators, but rather to arrest their victims and march them off to 'protective custody' in concentration camps. *Krystalnacht,* also known as 'The Night of Broken Glass' attracted worldwide condemnation. As with other aspects of the German experience with concentration camps, the British had already been there and in this case watched a version of 'The Night of Broken Glass' unfold in their own cities twenty-three years earlier.

In Liverpool on 10 May 1915, angry crowds attacked shops belonging to people with German names. Some of the owners of these shops had been living in Britain for fifty years and had sons serving in the British army, but it made no difference to the furious mobs. Houses were looted and what could not be carried away was thrown into the street and set on fire. Similar scenes took place across the country; from London to Salford. The reaction of the authorities was revealing. As the *Manchester Guardian* reported on 11 May, apropos of the rioting in Liverpool:

A great many Austrians and Germans in the city who have hitherto been allowed their liberty are now, it is stated, to be interned in order that they may be preserved from mob violence.

A few days later, columns of civilians were being marched out of the city under military escort. Their destination? A concentration camp.

Two days after the rioting, the Chief Constable of Manchester ordered the arrest of every German shopkeeper in the city. Similar actions were taken elsewhere. The pretext for the rounding up of harmless butchers and tobacconists was precisely the same as that used by the Germans in the aftermath of *Krystalnacht*; the men were being taken into protective custody to save them from harm. Just as in 1938, few people, even in Germany itself, had believed that this was the true reason that the men were being arrested; neither did they in England in May, 1915. It was widely known that the arrests were really reprisals for the sinking of the passenger line *Lusitania*; the event which had triggered the rioting in the first place.

The expression, 'concentration camp' really only acquired negative connotations during and after the Second World War. British newspapers in 1914 and 1915 did not hesitate to talk of the concentration camps which were being set up throughout the country. The purpose of these camps was, more often than not, to concentrate in one place foreigners who might not be fully supportive of the British war effort. These men were almost exclusively German and Austrian, although there was also a leavening of Turks and Bulgarians. Many had lived in Britain for years; sometimes for many decades. There was no suggestion that they really posed any threat to British interests; it was enough that they had been born in an enemy country.

The Defence of the Realm regulations provided the legal framework for interning civilians from enemy countries, but it is likely that the government was not, at least at first, especially keen to implement such measures. Some Germans living in this country were young men of military age who might conceivably have wished to return to their own country at the outbreak of war to enlist in the German army and fight against the British. Most though had lived in Britain for years; often they were married to English women and in some cases had become naturalised British citizens. They were pork butchers, waiters, bakers and jewellers who had no more desire to see a German victory than anybody else living in the United Kingdom. Such was the popular feeling and almost hysterical fear of spies and saboteurs, that the authorities thought it prudent to cater for the ordinary person's prejudices and arrest some of these innocent men; sending them to concentration camps.

At the outbreak of war in 1914, an old factory stood derelict in East London. William Ritchie and Sons had run a jute factory in Carpenter's

Road in Stratford; not far from where the Olympic stadium now stands. There was a fairly substantial community of Germans in East London at this time. They tended to be shopkeepers and there were so many of them in Stratford that it was known sometimes as Little Germany. The Germans had integrated well into the area and it was not until the war began that any sort of friction had been known in Stratford between the English and Germans. However, one way of demonstrating patriotism in the opening months of the war was by boycotting any business which was supposedly run by or owned by Germans. Rumours spread about anybody with a foreign-sounding name that they were secretly Germans. So bad did the situation become that some traders began to take out advertisements in local newspapers, declaring that they were British. Staddon and Sons, who ran drapers' shops in Plaistow and Barking, had a large advertisement published, in which they detailed their ancestry, pointing out that:

I should have supposed that there was no British who could not see with half an eye that the name STADDON was essentially English. 'English of the English'. As matter of fact, I was born in 'Glorious Devon', where my parents and forefathers had farmed for generations and with the single exception of a day trip to Cherbourg in a Channel Steamer, which I once took during a summer visit to the seaside, there is NO RECORD OF ONE OF US EVER HAVING BEEN OUT OF COUNTRY.

There were however other shopkeepers in East London whose antecedents were not so conspicuously British and on 15 December, a large number of these men were arrested by the police and marched to the disused jute factory in Carpenter's Road.

The Stratford Concentration Camp, for such was its official title, had a bad reputation among those interned during the First World War. Surrounded with barbed wire and with mounted machine guns pointing down at the prisoners, it was a grim place to spend the three years that it was in existence. Writing of it in his autobiography, *The London Years*, Rudolf Rocker wrote that:

The Stratford Camp and its Commandant had a dreadful reputation among the internees. News had spread of terrible things happening there. It was not always the fault of the British military administration. The German internal administration was as much to blame, particularly for a great deal of corruption which existed there. The head of the internal administration was man named Weber, who seemed by all accounts to be a sadist and did his best to make life in the camp impossible. We were told about a Sergeant Trinneman at Stratford, who was the Commandant's right-hand man and practically ran the camp. He was said to be a brute.

Those who are familiar with accounts of the concentration camps of the Third Reich will find descriptions such as the one above, eerily familiar. The *kapos*, prisoners in positions of trust and authority in Nazi camps, were often said to be even more cruel and sadistic than their German masters. So it was at the British concentration camps during the First World War. The commandants would choose prisoners and place them in authority over the others. This power often went to the men's heads.

There was certainly casual brutality at the Stratford Camp. One hundred and forty prisoners there signed a complaint against the Commandant, a career soldier. One man to whom he was speaking refused to address the commandant as 'Sir', for which impudence he was struck in the face by the commandant.

It is strange that the memory of these concentration camps, established not in remote rural areas, but in the very heart of the British capital, should have faded so completely. You would be hard-pressed to find a local resident in that part of London who has even the vaguest idea that a concentration camp was once operating only a few streets from where they live. An even more extraordinary example of such convenient amnesia concerns the concentration camp which was set up at a major London landmark.

Alexandra Palace is an entertainment venue in North London. Opened in 1873 as a centre for entertainment and education, it lies between the suburbs of Muswell Hill and Wood Green. Alexandra Palace is famous as being the site of the world's first 'high definition' television broadcasts, which the BBC began in 1936. 'Ally Pally', as it is known affectionately to the locals, was perfect for broadcasting, being situated on a tall hill, with a commanding view across the whole of London. BBC news broadcasts continued from Alexandra Palace until 1969 and Open University programmes went out from there until the 1980s.

Ask anybody living in and around the area about the history of Alexandra Palace and you will be sure to pick up snippets of history of this sort. You will also be told of the two huge fires which almost destroyed the place; once in 1875 and again in 1980. You might even hear of the supposed 'gypsy's curse' legend associated with these fires. Some know that there was once a racecourse there. One thing you will not be told, because it has been entirely lost to memory, is that a century ago, Alexandra Palace was the site of one of the largest concentration camps which this country has ever known; holding over 3,000 prisoners.

At the outbreak of war in 1914, Alexandra Palace was commandeered by the military and used as the headquarters for King Edward's Horse. The horses were kept at times in the tennis courts. Later, it was used to house refugees from Belgium. In March 1915, a concentration camp was established at Alexandra Palace for so-called 'enemy aliens'. These were Austrians and Germans who had been living in the United Kingdom when the war began. Many of them had been living in the country for years; some had arrived as babes in arms and knew no other home. Nevertheless, such men were technically German or Austrian, even if they could not speak a single word of German.

Sensitive to complaints of ill treatment, the British allowed both newspaper reporters and also representatives of the American embassy to visit Alexandra Palace and see for themselves the conditions that prevailed in the camp. On 21 May 1915, officials from the US embassy recorded that there were 1,286 German prisoners and another 100 from Austria. The Camp Commandant was Lieutenant-Colonel R.S.F. Walker.

Despite the fact that Germany was accusing the British of mistreating the prisoners at Alexandra Palace, there was little evidence of this, either in the accounts of the prisoners themselves or those who visited the camp to check on the conditions there. It was certainly no holiday camp; as new prisoners swelled the ranks, the place became horribly overcrowded.

The 3,000 men slept on plank beds in the great hall and on one occasion when the weather was foggy, the windows and doors remained closed for four days. The stench of so many human bodies crammed together was said to be abominable. The advantage of so many men in such close proximity was that despite the poor ventilation, the hall in which they all slept was never cold. Even in the middle of winter, it was generally as warm as anybody could wish.

Staff from the American embassy made several visits to the concentration camp at Alexandra Palace, to keep an eye on how things were developing there. In November 1916, the German leader of the camp told embassy officials that he and his fellow prisoners were quite satisfied with their treatment, food and accommodation and had no complaints to make. Others were not so completely content with the circumstances which they were forced to endure in the camp. Food was a particular source of anger among some men. The same buckets which were used for mopping the floor were used at mealtimes for serving up soup; a fact which made some prisoners unable to stomach the meal. In the later years of the war, horse meat was substituted for beef and the daily calorie intake for each man was estimated to have fallen to 1,489. The average man needs 2,500 calories a day simply to maintain his weight and health. These figures suggest that the prisoners at Alexandra Palace were, at least by 1918, on a starvation diet.

To get some idea of the kind of people who were caught up in the mania to intern anybody of German ancestry, we might look at father and son: Georg and Rudolf Sauter. Georg Sauter was a young Bavarian artist who came to London in 1889, at the age of 23. He spent a lot of time in the National Gallery, where he one day met Lilian Galsworthy; sister of the Nobel Prize winning author of *The Forsythe Saga*. Sauter married Galsworthy's sister and they soon had a son, whom they name Rudolf. When the First World War began, Georg Sauter had been living in England for twenty-five years and also had a 20-year-old son with very little experience of Germany, other than visiting the country on holidays. In all that time, Georg Sauter had never quite got round to becoming a naturalised British citizen. It was a lapse that was to cost him and his family dear, for both father and son were arrested and sent to the camp at Alexandra Palace. It was a terrible injustice which rankled in Georg Sauter's heart. When the war ended, he returned to Germany and remained there for the rest of his life.

The men who were detained at Alexandra Palace might have faced a meagre and unappetising diet, but at some concentration camps, they were being killed by rifle fire. The Isle of Man was thought to be the ideal location for keeping large numbers of prisoners, because of course anybody escaping would still find himself trapped on the island. Thousands of prisoners of war and civilian internees were held in camps on the island. On 19 November, there was a serious incident at the Douglas Alien Concentration Camp, as a result of which six men died.

There had been a number of complaints from the civilians who had been transferred to the concentration camp at Douglas from the mainland. These men were waiters, shopkeepers and so on and the only reason that they had been arrested was that they might be tempted at some point either to spy for their country of birth or to return to Germany to serve in that country's armed forces. The accommodation at Douglas was in tents and as winter approached, the prisoners felt these to be wholly inadequate for their needs. The food too left something to be desired.

On 5 November 1914, the weather in the Isle of Man was extremely wet and windy and the prisoners protested that they could not possibly be expected to stay in tents at such a time. After they had refused to enter their tents that night, there was a confrontation, which was resolved by the Commandant of the camp allowing some of them to sleep in the dining room; inside a brick building.

Dissatisfaction about the food provided grew stronger as November passed and on 19 November, the prisoners decided to stage a protest in the dining hall. After they had finished their midday meal, the men began to smash the crockery and overturn tables; jeering and booing at the kitchen staff. Guards were called and when they entered the dining hall, intending to disperse the protesting prisoners, they were met with a hail of food, pieces of broken crockery and the occasional chair. The situation at this point was rowdy and disorderly, rather than dangerous. If the guards had simply withdrawn and waited for the men to cool down, matters would most likely have passed without violence. In the event, they loaded their rifles and began firing into the dining hall.

That the guards at the Douglas Concentration Camp were intent upon carrying out a massacre seems beyond all reasonable doubt. Counting the remaining ammunition after the firing had ended and the dead and wounded removed from the scene, revealed that a total of thirty-four shots had been fired into the packed dining hall. Not one of the soldiers who began shooting in this disorganised fashion was later able to say who had given the order to open fire. A number of those who gave evidence at the subsequent inquest though were sure that *somebody* had told them to begin shooting into the packed dining hall.

Five men were killed immediately by the volleys of fire that day and another died later of his wounds. Many suffered bullet wounds and given the circumstances, it is a miracle that more did not die. The inquest, which was held the following month, found that the dead men were the victims of justifiable homicide, the protest in the dining hall having by that time been described in British newspapers as a, 'riot'.

This was not the only instance of a prisoner in a concentration camp being shot dead by guards. A few days before the shooting on the Isle of Man, there had been another incident, a little closer to London. One of the earliest camps to be set up for the internment of Germans and Austrians was at Camberley in Surrey. There were already 8,000 inmates on the middle of November 1914, when there was some sort of disturbance one night.

At about midnight, one of the guards at Camberley heard the sound of running feet and then some scuffling. When a light was turned onto the source of the sound, it became apparent that a group of prisoners were making towards one of the gates. After shouting a warning, the guards opened fire, killing one man and wounding another. It turned out that this was nothing more sinister than a few men brawling, after an argument got out of hand. It was not the concerted effort to rush the gates and overpower the sentries, that had been feared.

The mania for internment of enemy aliens went through waves. In between these crazes for persecuting harmless shopkeepers and artists, the authorities would sometimes release prisoners or deport them to neutral countries such as Holland. However, there were times when public opinion became so inflamed on this subject that it was necessary for the government to act to placate the demands of the public. This happened in the early summer of 1915, when the first phase of the enthusiasm for internment had died down.

By the early summer of 1915, many of those who had been rounded up at the start of the war had been quietly released. It was perfectly clear to anybody but a complete fool that German-born pork butchers from London's East End or waiters from seaside hotels really posed no sort of threat to the British nation. Although some younger men of military age were still detained, the rush to round up 'aliens' had largely subsided by the middle of 1915. This changed abruptly on the afternoon of 7 May 1915.

The world's largest and fastest passenger liner at that time, RMS *Lusitania*, was a British merchant ship. On Saturday 1 May, it had sailed from New York, heading for Liverpool. On board were 1,257 passenger and a 702-strong crew. Nobody seriously expected the Germans to attack merchant shipping; even if, as in this case, the ship was sailing under the British flag. The *Lusitania* was just ten miles from the Irish coast and almost at its destination when Kapitanleutnant Walter Schieger, the commander of the German submarine U-20, ordered the firing of a single torpedo at the mighty vessel. The *Lusitania* sank just 18 minutes later with the loss of almost 1,200 lives.

The response to the sinking of the *Lusitania* was swift and violent. The first rioting broke out in Liverpool; the home town of many of the liner's crew. The *Manchester Guardian* gave an account of the disturbances in its edition of Tuesday, 11 May 1915. The article began:

The rage and grief occasioned in Liverpool by the destruction of the Lusitania led to serious rioting in that city on Saturday, Sunday and yesterday. The premises of German tradesmen were attacked by large and angry crowds of men, women and children and the police had the greatest difficulty in coping with the outbreak. Indeed, in several instances, they were quite unable to disperse the crowds until serious damage had been done. A great many Germans and Austrians in the

city who have hitherto been allowed their liberty are now, it is stated,
to be interned so that they may be preserved from mob violence.

Shops were looted and the belongings of the owners burned, windows
smashed and anybody of German origin assaulted. The police could not
cope with the rioting and it was rumoured that the army would be called
in to tackle the situation, if it deteriorated further.

The next day, rioting spread to the south of England, with over 100 shops
and houses in East London being attacked, looted and sometimes burned. A
footnote in the newspapers informed readers that all German shopkeepers
in Manchester had now been arrested and taken to concentration camps
for their own safety. Writing of the aftermath of the riots in Liverpool,
the *Manchester Guardian* had this to say:

Hundreds of Germans have been lodged in the main bridewell and
there is scarcely an alien enemy at large in the city. The bridewell,
large as it is, has been found inadequate to accommodate all the aliens,
and removals are being made to concentration camps at Hawick and
elsewhere.

There is a modern expression for developments of this kind, where a specific
ethnic or national minority is driven from cities, locked in concentration
camps and then later deported from the country. It is ethnic cleansing.
This may sound like something of an exaggeration, until we look at the
figures involved. In the 1911 census, 31,254 German-born residents had
been recorded in the County of London; that part of the city excluding
the outer suburbs. By 1921, this figure had fallen to 9,083. In 1911, there
had been 8,869 Austrian born people in the same district; by 1921, there
were only 1,552.

The calls for the internment of 'enemy aliens' in concentration camps
continued on and off for the whole of the war. There were renewed
demands in 1918, following the bombing of London by German air
raids and reverses in the field on the Western Front. In the summer
of 1918, the very year that the war ended, there were mass rallies in
London, calling for any Germans still at liberty to be arrested and sent

to concentration camps. On 13 July 1918, an enormous rally was held in London's Trafalgar Square. It was said to be the biggest meeting held there since the war had begun. Messages were read out from people as varied and disparate as music hall star Harry Lauder and Rudyard Kipling, author of *The Jungle Book*. All called for the immediate internment of all Germans, men and women; whether they were naturalised British citizens or not.

Next month, a parade took place from Hyde Park to Downing Street, for the purpose of delivering a petition containing over a million signatures calling for the internment of all Germans and Austrians. The government, mindful of the fact that as soon as the war had ended, there would be a general election, conceded to these demands; setting up a new Enemy Aliens Advisory Committee. The task of this body was to examine all those of German and Austrian origin who had so far been given exemption from internment. In addition to revoking the naturalisation of some Germans who had become British citizens, deportations to Holland were stepped up. In September 1918, over 200 men a week were being taken from the concentration camps, shipped across the channel and dumped, penniless, in Holland.

We have looked at concentration camps operating in England and Wales during the Great War. It is now time to examine the situation in Scotland and to look at altogether different sorts of camp which were being run in that country from 1916 onwards.

3. The Home Office Work Camps

After the dissolution of the camp at Frongoch, it might have been assumed that there was no further appetite in Britain for the detention of its own citizens for political reasons. In general this was true and is still so; very few people in this country today would be in favour of indefinite detention without trial for purely political offences. There was in the middle of the First World War though an exception to this rule. This concerned a class of men who were so depraved and unnatural that nothing was thought too bad for them. These individuals deserved the strongest condemnation and harshest treatment and hardly anybody, other than a handful of cranks such as the philosopher Bertrand Russell, had a good word to say for them. Sending these men to concentration camps and forcing them to undertake backbreaking labour was thought to be almost too good for them.

Traditionally, the British army and navy had been composed entirely of volunteers. With the exception of the occasional aberration such as the press gangs which operated in some ports in the eighteenth and early nineteenth centuries, the only men serving in the British forces were those who chose to do so. All this changed during the war which began in 1914. So horrific were the losses on the Western Front that the supply of volunteers was not sufficient to replenish the heavily depleted units struggling to hold the line against Germany. At first, it was hoped to avoid compulsion by means of what became known as the Derby Scheme. This was devised by Lord Derby and implemented in October 1915. Those men who were willing to serve at some future time of need could register with the military authorities and attest to their willingness to be called up. They would then return to their ordinary work and wait to see if they were needed. Neither this nor the periodic recruiting drives, featuring a man at whose activities we have already looked, the new Minister for War, Lord Kitchener, were sufficient to raise the enormous numbers of men needed if Britain was to prevail against Germany and the Austro-Hungarian and Ottoman Empires. After all, by 1916, British casualties were running at around half a million.

The wartime coalition government contained many Liberals who were appalled at the idea of compulsory military service, but despite this, the Military Service Act became law in 1916 and required all single men resident in Britain and between the ages of 18 and 41, to join the army. Later that same year, the act was extended to include married men. In this way, a total of five million men were conscripted into the armed forces. It must be remembered that there was no necessity for a man to receive his call-up papers or report to some base in order to be considered an enlisted soldier. On the day that the Military Service Act came into force, which was Thursday, 2 March 1916, every man living in Britain who was unmarried and between the ages of 18 and 41 was automatically enlisted into the armed forces and so subject to military law.

Such was the popular enthusiasm for the war, that hardly any of those called up raised any objection. Legal considerations apart, social disapproval of such objectors was powerful and those hesitating to serve their country in this was were castigated as 'slackers' and 'shirkers'.

Some men however had deep-seated and indeed overwhelming reasons for refusing to be drafted into the army. These men were the conscientious objectors and they were almost universally reviled. While everybody else's husbands, brothers and sons were doing their bit and risking their lives, these cowards simply said that they did not wish to go to war and preferred to stay safely at home. It is hard now to realise just how strong was the popular feeling against such men.

Despite the enormous unpopularity of those who wished to 'dodge the column', as the saying was at that time, the government had made provision for men who really had religious, ethical or philosophical objections to being in the army. It was possible to apply for a certificate of exemption if, according to the words of the act, a man had a 'conscientious objection to the undertaking of combatant service'. This was the only reference to the subject in the act and it was left to the Military Service Tribunals who were responsible for issuing certificates of exemption to decide for themselves how to interpret the law.

Only a tiny number of men registered as having a conscientious objection to fighting. Out of five million who were enlisted, a mere 16,500 applied to Military Service Tribunals for exemption certificates on the basis that they were conscientious objectors. This works out at 0.3 per cent of those called up for military service.

It soon became apparent that the men applying for exemption certificates on the grounds of conscience could be divided into three categories. There were those who were prepared to join the army and wear uniforms, always provided that they were not expected to carry or use weapons. These were the easiest to deal with and a Non-Combatant Corps was set up in the army for them. Some worked as stretcher bearers, others did manual work. All were exposed to the same risk of death as other soldiers and were accorded a certain amount of grudging respect. Then there were the 'alternativists', who would perform other work of national importance, as long as it was not under military control. The final group were the most difficult to deal with. These were the 'absolutists', who were so bitterly opposed to the war that they would do nothing at all which might aid the war effort.

If a tribunal refused to issue a man with a certificate of exemption, then he was technically enlisted in the army and subject to military law. If he did not report for service, then he could be arrested by the military police and court-martialled. In practice, such men were usually sent to civil prisons to serve any sentence of imprisonment, although there were cases when the army chose to treat them as being mutinous soldiers, rather than misguided civilians. In the most notorious such case, thirty-five conscientious objectors were taken by the army to France and informed that as they were now in the presence of the enemy, any refusal to obey orders would be a capital crime. Because this motley collection of Quakers, Methodists and Jehovah's Witnesses still would not do as they were told, they were court-martialled and sentenced to be shot at dawn. The sentences were commuted to ten years imprisonment and they were returned to England, where they were sent to ordinary prisons.

The British prison system was becoming clogged up with hundreds and then thousands of men who were not criminals in any real meaning of the word and as the months passed, it became clear that some other system would be needed to deal with such men. A committee was set up under the leadership of William Brace; a Labour MP and Under-Secretary at the Home Office and a scheme devised which, it was thought, might solve the problem. The Brace Committee recommended the setting up of 'work centres', where absolutists might be employed in conditions which would be as arduous as those being endured by men at the front. It was guessed, quite rightly, that among the genuine idealists who were ready to suffer imprisonment for their beliefs, there might be others who were simply hoping to wait out the war safely in a prison cell. This was without doubt the view of many members of the public, who were outraged to think that while their relatives were risking death in France, these shirkers were sitting in warm cells; certain to survive the war. A tough regime of hard labour could persuade such men that they might as well be at the front with everybody else.

The Brace Committee came up with the idea of Work Centres and Home Office Camps. These were to be places where conscientious objectors could be sent to, rather than to leave them in prison. Conditions at such centres were meant to be tough and work undertaken was supposed to be gruelling. The first two work centres were set up at Wakefield in Yorkshire and Princetown in Devon. Camps were also set up in Scotland, to which men from England would be sent.

Wakefield and Princetown were of course the locations of prisons which had long been established. The ordinary criminal prisoners were removed and the two gaols prepared for the new influx of men sentenced to two years or more imprisonment for refusing to obey military orders.

Wakefield and Princeton, more commonly known as Dartmoor, were relatively comfortable; at least they were warm and dry. The same could not be said for the camps to which the conscientious objectors were to be sent. Before looking in detail at the conditions in one of those camps in particular, perhaps we should bear in mind that not all those men who were avoiding military service were motivated by high-minded principles. Some at least were simply ordinary men who did not wish to be shipped off to France to become cannon-fodder on the Western Front. It was partly to deter men of this type that conditions were made so harsh in the work camps.

Herbert Watters was a blacksmith whose family lived on the Gower Peninsular of Wales. When he was called up in 1916, he claimed that the two forges that he was running were work of national importance and that he should not therefore be conscripted. The Gower Rural Military Service tribunal rejected this notion and ordered Watters to report for service. He refused and in October 1916, found himself at the Swansea Magistrates' Court. He was fined £2 and handed over to the military police, who took Herbert Watters to his unit; the 60th Training Reserve Battalion. The idea was that after receiving some initial training, Watters would be sent to France. He however, had other ideas. His military service record was filled out at the camp on 14 October 1916 and two days later he was facing a court martial for refusing to obey orders.

There was never at any time the least suggestion that Herbert Watters was motivated by idealism. He was just a bloody-minded and awkward individual who was determined not to be conscripted into the army and then sent to fight the Germans. He was sentenced at court martial to six months' imprisonment with hard labour and sent to Wormwood Scrubs Prison to complete his sentence. The army must have decided by now that having such a man in their ranks would be more trouble than it was worth, because on 16 December 1916, Watters was released from prison and transferred to the Army Reserve so that he could, 'undertake work of national importance under the direction of the Brace Committee'. In effect, Herbert Watters had won. He would not be sent to France and was merely to spend the war doing manual labour.

After being sent to a road-work camp in Argyleshire in Scotland, Watters found to his surprise that he was given command of a forge and expected to resume his work as a blacksmith, repairing the tools of those building the road. Later, he was sent to Glencoe and then Wakefield Prison. It was because it was very well known that among those refusing to be conscripted were men like this, that conditions at the Home Office work camps were sometimes made as harsh as possible. It was felt that if things were bad enough, then such men would give up and agree to serve in the army.

A notoriously bad camp established by the Brace Committee was operating on the outskirts of Aberdeen from August to October 1916. There was a granite quarry at Dyce and the intention was that men at the camp would labour there; breaking stones to be used in road building. From late August onwards, men began to arrive at Dyce Camp from the prisons where they had been held. Eventually, 250 men were living at Dyce; the majority accommodated in leaky, draughty tents dating from the Boer War. The camp was set up on sloping ground, which meant that when it rained, water ran down the hillside and into the tents. Whether this was accidental or planned in order to make conditions even more unpleasant for the inmates of the camp, considerable discomfort was caused by the damp which pervaded the tents. They slept on straw mattresses which were placed directly on the wet ground.

Most of these men were objecting to war on religious grounds or because they were pacifists. They were in civilian life teachers, clerks and white-collar workers, wholly unused to labouring, and yet were now expected to work hard for ten hours a day in a quarry. This, combined with the draughty tents and damp conditions, had an exceedingly poor effect upon the health of some. This was neatly illustrated soon after the camp was set up, when on 8 September, a 20-year-old man called Walter Roberts died of pneumonia. It was claimed that the Dyce Work Camp was being run in a punitive fashion which was likely to lead to further deaths. Letters from inmates alleged that many more men were falling ill and that it was a matter of time before others died of pneumonia.

Ramsay McDonald, the Scottish-born leader of the Labour Party visited Dyce in October 1916 and was shocked at what he saw there. In a speech to the House of Commons on 19 October, he described the terrible living conditions at the camp and the high levels of illness. The Home Office was not happy to have attention drawn to their camps in this way and Dyce was quietly closed down that same month.

After the scandal at Dyce Camp was revealed, the government quietly made the remaining Home Office Camps a little less harsh. They had already received enough bad publicity from the concentration camps that they had been running in England and Wales and with all sides in the First World War eagerly spreading atrocity stories, it was perhaps felt that there was no point courting any further bad publicity in this way. Rumours were spreading about the work-camps, which were being described in some quarters as concentration camps. The stories, circulating by word of mouth, hinted that dogs were being used to guard the prisoners at such camps and that conditions at some were even worse than they were at Dyce.

Conscientious objectors may have been the least popular and most reviled group of men in the country, but there were limits to how ordinary people felt that they should be treated. With the increasing awareness of places such as Frongoch and Dyce, the feeling began to grow that it was a bit much to confine British citizens in such places. There was no objection to keeping thousands of men of German and Austrian ancestry in concentration camps, but it was not really the thing for our own people.

Chapter Four

1929-1939
'Work Sets you Free': The British Labour
Camps of the Inter-war Years

Wrought in iron above the gates of Dachau, the first concentration camp in Nazi Germany, were the words, 'ARBEIT MACHT FREI'. In German, this means, literally, 'Work makes free'. The implication is that work will bring as its reward, freedom. This same slogan was later placed over the entrance to Auschwitz and it has been widely assumed that this was a fiendish black joke on the part of the SS, in that they knew very well that there was not the slightest possibility of any of the slave labourers in the camps being made free by their work. In fact it is altogether possible that rather than being placed there cynically, as a taunt to the prisoners, this phrase was used quite honestly by those who set up the camps and that it expressed some mystical reverence for the idea of physical work.

The expression 'Arbeit macht frei' was not dreamed up by the Nazis, but was actually a slogan of the Weimar Republic, which preceded the Third Reich. Even they did not invent the wording, which is the title of a German novel published in 1873. The book, by Lorenz Diefenbach, tells of the redemption of a group of dissolute gamblers by honest, hard work. This concept, that there is something virtuous and liberating about physical work for its own sake was common in the middle of the twentieth century and lingers on to this day. Unemployment is, even now, sometimes seen as undesirable not simply because it reduces men to poverty, but because the enforced idleness which goes hand in hand with unemployment is viewed as a moral evil, which saps the vitality and worth of those without jobs; leading them on a downwards path which is likely to end in apathy and vice. From this perspective, being without work is bad in itself and society should do all it can to remedy the state of affairs.

The concentration camps at which we have so far looked were described as such at the time and involved an element of compulsion. Few people would choose to be detained in such places. The labour camps set up and run in remote rural parts of Britain from 1929 until the outbreak of war in the summer of 1939 were a little different. They were, at least in theory, voluntary establishments, from which any of the inmates could walk out whenever they pleased. There was however a good deal more to it than that. Despite their supposedly voluntary nature, there were eerie similarities between them and the camps set up in Germany at the same time by the Nazis. The idea of both was that men should be reclaimed through honest labour and that those who had hitherto led idle or vicious lives could redeem themselves through hard, purely physical work. Like the concentration camps in Germany, the British labour camps were all in remote areas and few people knew of their existence. Even today, hardly anybody has heard of them.

A word here about the loaded nature of an expression such as 'labour camps' might be in order. If concentration camps are inextricably linked in the average person's mind with Nazi Germany, then labour camps are automatically associated with Soviet Russia. This reflex connection of different kinds of camps with particular countries has only emerged since the end of the Second World War. The term 'labour camp' had few negative connotations during the 1930s and was widely used both in parliament and the press. The British camps of that period will accordingly be referred to here as labour camps; which is what they indubitably were.

Few readers will be unfamiliar with the image of poor, starved Oliver Twist in the workhouse, saying, 'Please sir, I want some more.' The institution of the workhouse is understood by everybody today to have been a bad one; we rightly believe such places to have been little better than prisons. This is of course perfectly true, but we should also bear in mind that in theory they were, unlike prisons, completely voluntary establishments. Nobody was confined in the workhouse and the inmates were free to leave at any time. Nevertheless, hardly anybody ever walked out, for the same reason that those in the labour camps of the 1930s did not in general leave.

Until the passing of the *Poor Law Amendment Act of 1834*, more commonly known as the New Poor Law, those in England who were poverty stricken due to unemployment could apply for help from the parish in which they lived. This was often provided in the form of 'outdoor relief'; money or food distributed to the poor, who remained living in their own homes. From 1795 onwards, this developed into what became known as the 'Speenhamland System'; named after the town of Speen in Berkshire. Assistance was calculated according to both the price of bread and the number of children in a family. Even those who were working were eligible for relief of this sort, which was roughly analogous to today's supplementary benefit. The system was expensive, being paid from the local rates, and open to abuse. Employers, for instance, would pay lower wages, knowing that their workers could claim relief from the parish which would make up any shortfall in wages.

After 1834, outdoor relief became rare and those who were so poverty-stricken that they were unable to survive had, as their only option, to ask to be allowed to enter the workhouse. Conditions in the workhouses were deliberately made as grim and unattractive as possible. It was intended that the standard of living in such places was to be lower than anywhere outside the workhouse. The rationale behind this was to make the workhouse an unattractive prospect for the work-shy and idle. Once there, families were split up, with men living separately from their wives, and children being housed apart from their parents. Inmates wore a degrading uniform and were expected to work for their food, by picking oakum, for example.

Although those in workhouses could leave at any time if they wished, many faced the prospect of starvation if they did so. In 1844, the government passed the Outdoor Relief Prohibitory Order, which tightened up the system still further and ensured that no aid was offered to the unemployed or poor, other than by their entering the workhouse. Since the alternative to the workhouse could literally be death, it is debatable whether or not we can really say that those living in these institutions were there voluntarily.

Surprisingly, workhouses were not officially abolished until the passing of the 1929 Local Government Act, which came into force on 1 April 1930. Even then, some workhouses were renamed Public Assistance Institutions and continued operating for another decade. As late as 1939, the year that the Second World War began, there were still 100,000 people, including over 5,000 children in such establishments.

At about the same time that the workhouses were being abolished, a Labour government led by Ramsay McDonald was getting to grips with the effects of the Great Depression. This gloomy period of economic stagnation gripped the world from 1930 until roughly the end of World War Two. In some parts of Britain, unemployment rose to shocking levels; 30 per cent of workers in Glasgow were out of work at the height of the depression. This was roughly the figure for south Wales as a whole. Unemployment was worst in industrial and mining areas; south Wales, the north of England and other such places. In some places, almost every man was out of work. The unemployment rate in the Welsh town of Taff's Well was 82 per cent. In the south of Britain, things were much better and agriculture was experiencing a boom during the 1930s. Factories such as those manufacturing motor cars were also booming; in stark contrast to the shipyards of the north of England. If only some of those unemployed miners and factory workers could be persuaded to move away from the so-called 'distressed areas' and go where there were jobs to be found in the rural economy and factories of south east England, it was thought by those in government that much of the suffering could be alleviated.

Even without any government initiatives to encourage the movement of workers from the depressed areas, many families moved to more prosperous locations where work *was* available. Between 1921 and 1940, some 440,000 people left Wales; 85 per cent of them from Glamorgan and Monmouthshire, where unemployment was highest.

In many ways, the situation in Britain during the Great Depression of the thirties was precisely the opposite of that faced by the country in 1834, when the New Poor Law had come into effect. At that time, as the Industrial Revolution gathered pace, the aim had been to get unemployed rural workers from the countryside to seek jobs in the new factories being opened in the Midlands and north of England. One objective of the 1834 law had been to encourage this shift from the countryside to the town. Now, in the aftermath of the Wall Street Crash, it was thought that some of Britain's difficulties could be overcome if all those people standing idly on the street corners of Manchester, Glasgow and various Welsh mining towns could somehow be transported to farms and given jobs as agricultural labourers. The problem was of course that they stubbornly insisted on remaining where they were and did not have any desire at all to leave the districts where they had grown up and where all their family and friends were living. They would need to be given a nudge.

When Ramsay McDonald formed a minority Labour government in the summer of 1929, he appointed the first ever woman to the cabinet. Margaret Bondfield was 56 and had previously been a junior minister in McDonald's 1924 administration. Now, she was given the post of Minister of Labour. At that time, unemployment was already a serious problem; over a million people were either on the dole or claiming unemployment benefit. The previous Conservative government under Stanley Baldwin had tinkered with the problem of long-term unemployment which afflicted certain areas, but without any noticeable result. Now, the new Minister for Labour was determined to tackle the scourge head on.

Under the Conservatives, a number of centres had been set up to retrain men and equip them with the skills which might enable them to be more attractive to potential employers. Those who were claiming the dole were invited to attend these institutions. There was a marked reluctance among the unemployed to travel miles to stay in residential centres, as this would mean leaving their friends and family behind. Margaret Bondfield had no patience for pussyfooting around the question and told the cabinet on 23 December 1929 that she wished to remove any choice in the matter and compel men to go and live in what were now being termed 'Transfer Instructional Centres'. She said at the cabinet meeting that day that she was most concerned about men who were unlikely to obtain work without a 'course of reconditioning', and referred bitterly to those who refused 'to avail themselves of the offer of training'.

There sounds something a little sinister about the idea of 'reconditioning' men, but Bondfield was not the only person in the Ministry of Labour who was using this expression. A year earlier, F.G. Bowers, a civil servant in the Ministry of Labour, had prepared a memo in which he talked of unemployed men who had gone 'soft' and of the need for them to be 'hardened' at special centres.

It is time to look at what these Transfer Instructional Centres, later called simply Instructional Centres, actually were. To all intents and purposes, they were labour camps, where 'soft' men would be 'reconditioned' and 'hardened'. This process would be accomplished by means of rough living for a few months, during which the men would spend their days engaged in the heaviest kind of physical labour: digging ditches, breaking stones, felling trees and sawing timber. The camps were all in remote, out-of-the-way places and the intention was that after they had been reconditioned, it might be possible for the men to obtain work of this sort on the land, far from the areas of high unemployment from which they came.

Accommodation in the camps was basic, similar perhaps to that provided in army barracks. The food was adequate and filling; and the men sent there lived a life in many ways like that of soldiers. They were issued with heavy work clothes and cutlery and lived in wooden huts.

The compulsion used to get men to agree to leave their homes and live under fairly harsh conditions of this sort was simple, but devastatingly effective. Those who refused to take up a place at the camp to which they had been allocated would no longer be entitled to any unemployment benefit or dole. For men with families, this was a most potent means of persuasion, involving as it did the threat of hardship and even starvation for their wives and children.

Before looking in greater detail at life in the camps, it is instructive to compare what was happening in Britain with similar projects being undertaken in Nazi Germany at roughly the same time. On 21 March 1933, the office of Heinrich Himmler, head of the SS, issued a press release about a new facility which was being set up near Munich. Part of it read:

Communist functionaries, Reichsbanner and Marxist functionaries who threaten the security of the state will be assembled here. Leaving

> *individual Communist functionaries in the courthouse jails is not*
> *possible for the long term without putting too much strain on them*
> *apparatus of the state.*

Life in the new camp did not sound particularly disagreeable:

> *The Dachau camp consists of over 20 one to two-story stone buildings,*
> *each of which can hold 200 to 250 men. At first the occupancy of the*
> *camp will gradually increase to 2,500 men and will possibly be expanded*
> *to 5,000 men later. A labour service detachment recently prepared the*
> *barrack for the first 200 men and secured it for the time being with*
> *a barrier of triple barbed-wire. The first job of the camp inmates will*
> *be to restore the other stone buildings, which are very run-down. Once*
> *that is accomplished, they will be led out in small groups of about 50*
> *men into the countryside, where extensive land cultivation projects*
> *wait to be implemented. Perhaps later, some of the camp inmates will*
> *be offered the possibility of settling here.*

Reading through this account, there appear to be few differences between the regime at Dachau and that at the labour camps which were being opened, first by the Labour government and then later the National Government, in 1930s Britain. Just as in Britain, there was the idea that 'reconditioning' men might be good for them, combined with the possibility that they might wish to move to another part of the country and earn their daily bread in this way in the future. According to Himmler's office, this was just the sort of thing that was going on at the Third Reich's first concentration camp. After the inmates had learned how to work properly, these same men might even wish to stay at Dachau and settle on the land permanently!

As a matter of fact, there almost certainly were very few differences between Dachau and the British labour camps at that time. One person who visited Dachau concentration camp in 1936 and was very favourably impressed by what he saw was former British Prime Minister David Lloyd George. He talked enthusiastically of the virtues of good, honest labour and spoke of the men he had seen, stripped to their waists, who were digging ditches around the camp. For Lloyd George at least, the idea that 'Arbeit macht Frei' was a sound and desirable one.

Lloyd George was not the only British visitor to the German concentration camps to find the treatment of the inmates quite acceptable. On 4 October 1933, the *Manchester Guardian*, forerunner of today's *Guardian*, published a letter from Brigadier-General R.B.D. Blakeney; who had just recently returned from a visit to Germany, Brigadier Blakeney had on 13 September been shown round the Sonnenberg concentration camp, which was not far from the Polish border. The Brigadier found everything at Sonnenberg to be eminently satisfactory. He wrote:

The prisoners did not appear to be ill-treated, so much so that three who were just being released looked clean, healthy, and much improved by their regime of daily baths, regular meals, physical drill and discipline.

As far as Brigadier Blakeney was concerned, a couple of months in a concentration camp was roughly comparable to a spell in the army; an experience which was fundamentally beneficial to those subjected to it. In fact the descriptions that Lloyd George, Brigadier Blakeney and many others at that time give of the German concentration camps is practically indistinguishable from what unemployed men in the British labour camps would have been familiar with. Physical exercise, discipline, regular meals, daily baths and roughing it a little in wooden huts; who could possibly object to such a regime?

There can be no doubt that in the 1930s, both in Germany and Britain, there was a feeling that *arbeit* did indeed *macht frei*! Nothing like a spot of digging ditches and so on for toughening men up and making them fit to live once more in ordinary society. It is perhaps significant that while the British had named their camps 'Instructional Centres', the Germans at first intended that their own, similar, establishments should be known as 'Re-education Centres'. Whatever the name eventually chosen, the camps themselves were astonishingly similar.

At the time, the Instructional Centres were generally referred to by those being sent to them as work camps or labour camps. Some left-wing political groups denounced them as concentration camps. Plate 7 shows a leaflet in which the Instructional Centres were described in this way. This was a touchy point for those actually running the places; with the German camps beginning to acquire an unwholesome reputation for themselves, few officials in Britain wished to be thought of as connected with concentration camps. Even the word 'camp' was avoided wherever possible. In 1935, an official of the Unemployment Assistance Board was worried about the terminology being used by civil servants. He wrote:

Above all, the word 'camp' must never be applies to any open-air training schemes. The communist orators and pamphleteers have been quick to play upon unpleasant association of ideas by denouncing such organisations as 'Concentration Camps'.

It is time to look in detail at the extent to which the British camps could really be considered 'voluntary'. From 1930 onwards, Ramsay McDonald's government was doing everything possible to balance the budget. Exports were falling and unemployment rising steeply. It was thought that the only way to restore international confidence in the pound was to make savage cuts in public expenditure. This is a familiar problem today and the present British government is seeking to perform precisely the same surgery on public spending. Now as then, one area for savings is likely to be the benefits being paid to those on social security.

For Ramsay McDonald's administration, the financial crisis was infinitely worse than that faced by the recent Coalition government of Britain. Since unemployment benefits were soaring, the National Government hit firstly upon the idea of slashing all payments by 10 per cent and then taking steps to see if they could not avoid paying out money altogether to some families. This was the much hated 'means test'.

Those who had paid enough contributions under the *1911 Insurance Act* were entitled to claim six months unemployment benefit if they were out of work. These payments were unconditional and the means test was not applied to them. If a person was still unemployed after six months, then the *1921 Insurance Act* provided for further 'uncovenanted benefit'. These payments were given grudgingly and with reluctance; they were 'doled' out. Hence the use of the expression, 'the dole'. The benefits under this scheme were kept as low as possible by examining every aspect of the person's life; all savings and any source of income whatsoever were taken into account. When ordinary unemployment benefit was being claimed, a man's wife could be supplementing the family income by taking in washing or charring, the children might be doing paper rounds. When calculating the amount to hand out for the dole, any such income was measured and the payments made to the unemployed head of the family reduced accordingly. The aim was to give the absolute bare minimum which would keep body and soul together.

At first, the so-called 'dole' was distributed by the local Public Assistance Committees which had replaced the old Poor Law Guardians. In 1934, a National Assistance Board was created, which dictated to the last penny, exactly how much assistance should be offered to the unemployed.

This strict approach to the paying out of benefits may or may not have been good for the British economy as a whole. What is certain is that it left millions of people living on the edge of malnutrition. Government research during the 1930s suggested that about a quarter of the British population were at that time living on a subsistence diet, with dietary deficiencies common and resultant disorders such as rickets being endemic in some areas. In the 'Special Areas', such as South Wales, things were often far worse than in the rest of the country. There were epidemics of scarlet fever and the incidence of tuberculosis in Wales was running at 130 per cent higher than for the rest of the United Kingdom. A quarter of all Welsh miners between the ages of 25 and 34 had lost all their teeth.

It is in this context that we must look at the idea that going off to an Instructional Centre for three months was a voluntary undertaking. When a man, and sometimes his family, are on the verge of starvation and wholly dependent on state benefits, then the threat of withdrawing those benefits entirely is a chilling one. The great majority of those 'offered' the chance of a spell in an instructional centre would probably have declined; all else being equal.

The focus of the efforts to 're-train' unemployed men were the four so-called 'special areas'; the north-east coast of England, west Cumberland, Scotland and South Wales. In these parts of Britain, unemployment was running throughout the 1930s at about 33 per cent. Half the men in those places had been without work for a year or more; in some cases, much longer than that. There was also widespread unemployment in other parts of the country; Manchester and the cities of the Midlands, for example. The slowdown in mining and industry meant that there was no realistic prospect of creating new jobs in these places. That being so, the logical solution was to move the unemployed men and their families to other parts of the United Kingdom where there *were* jobs.

This was one strand of the policy which saw the setting up of the labour camps. Another fear was that after being on the dole for years, many of these men had grown mentally and physically unfit for work. They were soft and flabby and the enforced idleness had sapped their morale; leaving them lazy and apathetic. What they needed was rousing and being given a bit of a shock to get them moving again. They also needed to be prepared psychologically for the idea that they might have to leave where they were currently living and move to the other end of the country. Most had previously worked in factories, mines and shipyards, but these kind of jobs were no longer available. Very well then, they must be shown how to do other kinds of work; the sort of work for which there *was* a demand. They would, in other words, have to go where the jobs were, rather than hang around the street corners of the towns in depressed areas; chatting and smoking with their pals.

This then was the theory behind the camps. It was, without doubt, a well-meaning effort on behalf of the government, although one doomed to failure. The fact is, people simply do not wish to uproot themselves and go to live somewhere where they know nobody, have no family or friends and work among a lot of strangers. This is still largely the case today, but in the 1930s such feelings were even stronger. Many people grew up, married, worked and raised their children just round the corner from where they had themselves been born and gone to school. It was not uncommon at that time for a man to live only a couple of streets away from his own parents and this was especially so in districts like the valleys of South Wales. The idea of being forced to move to Essex or Kent would have struck such men as unthinkable. It would have been a form of internal exile, the sort of thing that one would expect in the Soviet Union rather than Britain.

Still, with the alternative of losing all assistence from either the local parish or any state benefits, the men invited to join this scheme really had little choice. It was compulsion in all but name and over 200,000 men ended up unwillingly spending time in one of camps. Annual admissions to the Instructional Centres rose sharply from 1929, until over 23,000 men a year were being sent to them. Here are the annual figures for admission to the camps from 1929 to 1938:

1929	3,518
1930	9,886
1931	11,170
1932	16,540
1933	21,715
1934	22,788
1935	18,474
1936	24,146
1937	20,588
1938	23,772

The number of camps operating fluctuated from year to year, as new ones opened and others closed. At any one time though, there were about thirty running; each with the capacity to hold between 150 and 200 men. Almost without exception, they were built in remote areas; far away from villages and towns. There was no sinister reason for establishing them in isolated spots, it was simply that they were mostly built on land belonging to the Forestry Commission, which mean that they were bound to be in, or on the edges of, forests. This meant that there was plenty of outdoor labouring available for the men, which was, after all, the object of the exercise.

Most of those who ended up in the labour camps had worked only indoors or underground in factories and mines. Undertaking hard, physical work in the open air was a novel experience for them. The work varied between hauling and sawing up logs, to breaking stones in a quarry. The food provided was filling and nutritious. It was thought that many working class men had grown puny and undersized while out of work and the aim was to build up their bodies a little and make them fit for hard work again.

It has to be said that the regime in the camps was certainly not cruel or harsh. It was perhaps no tougher than being in the army for a few months. The men slept in corrugated-iron Nissen huts; fifteen or twenty to a hut. They were issued on arrival at the camp with cutlery, work clothes and bedding and were expected to keep their huts clean and tidy. Many of the instructors working at the camps were themselves ex-soldiers, often Sergeant-Majors, and there was an air of military discipline. The men in some camps were, for instance, marched to and fro in squads and ordered to parade for work in the morning. At night, a roll call was held to ensure that nobody had gone missing.

The course of instruction at the camps lasted for three months, which was a long time for men to be separated from their friends and family. They were however given a rail warrant to enable them to visit their homes once a month. Although there were attempts to provide recreation for the men, in the form of lectures, sports and so on; the focus, and ultimate purpose, of the camps was of course work.

One of the things that many men who spent their three-month periods at these camps remarked, was that the work appeared to be undertaken for its own sake and not really for the purpose of training anybody in anything useful. Stones were quarried and broken into small pieces with sledge hammers, so that they could be used for road building, tree trunks were sawn into sections, tree roots were dug up and land cleared. It was almost as though they were being made to undertake hard, physical labour for no other reason than to make them exhausted. There may well have been something in this. There was an official concern during the Depression that unemployed men were becoming 'soft' and 'flabby'. It was for this reason that they were to be 'reconditioned'; made fit and strong once more and ready to take up labouring jobs.

It is curious to note that unemployment and poverty are in Britain today, often associated with obesity. During the Great Depression; the case was quite different. The main concern about manual workers who were seeking work was that they were under-nourished and thin. On arrival at the camps, the men were weighed and the hope was that with the filling, carbohydrate-rich food which was provided, that they would put on weight. Any weight put on would be in the form of muscle and not fat. Work began at 6:00 am and typically lasted for ten or twelve hours. The men would be absolutely ravenous after such exertion and as much food as required could be eaten.

How successful was this scheme of social engineering? Did it help to move unemployed workers from the Special Areas and into those parts of the country where jobs were more plentiful? In fact, the Instructional centres failed on both counts. Hundreds of thousands of people moved from the Special Areas and obtained work elsewhere, but this was almost invariably as a result of personal initiative on the part of those concerned, rather than as a consequence of any government scheme. As far as the men who returned from their stint at a labour camp; their prospects remained as dismal as ever. Only 10 per cent of those who had spent their three months in an Instructional Centre went on to find work. It was the view of many who had spent time in such establishments, that going there had actually had the effect of *reducing* their chances of finding work. The reason was that news of jobs was often passed by word of mouth around the tightly-knit communities of the mining and manufacturing towns. Somebody's uncle or brother might recommend a man to a foreman taking on new workers or a mate might hear of some opportunity. Being sent hundreds of miles away for three months, removed a man from this informal but often highly effective sort of networking and he then missed any jobs which cropped up while he was away.

The British experiment with labour camps had not been a success and it is open to question whether the true aim of sending men to these places was really to help prepare them for working in the field of agriculture. It is by no means impossible that the system of camps was set up more to galvanise people into action and compel them to make some more effort of their own to find work. It would be wrong to describe them as being punitive, but there was perhaps a school of thought in London, among both cabinet ministers and civil servants, which held that much of the problem in the depressed parts of the country were due to idleness. Newsreel films showed unemployed miners standing around on street corners in South Wales; seemingly idling their time away in smoking and chatting to other men with nothing to do. Why weren't such men out looking actively for new work? Clearly, it was believed by some of those in authority, these were people who had just given up! They needed a bit of a shock and had to be given the incentive to pull themselves together again and help themselves.

This unspoken assumption, that the unemployed have a tendency to get used to a life on benefits and to stop looking for another job, is still a fairly common one today in certain official circles. Every so often, some politician will come up with an idea like 'workfare', where those claiming to be unable to find a job will be made to work publicly in order to earn their benefits. This sort of thing is not meant to be pleasant; it is supposed to serve as a wake-up call. It is into this category that we should perhaps place the Instructional Centres of the 1930s.

Chapter Five

1940-1946
They must have known!
The Polish Concentration Camps in Britain

At the end of the Second World War, when the full horrors of German concentration camps such as Dachau and Belsen were revealed, many civilians who had been living near to these dreadful establishments claimed that they had had no knowledge at all of what had been going on in them. The British and American armies forced the citizens of nearby towns to tour the camps, so that they could see for themselves what had been done in their name. Unable to believe that ordinary Germans had been oblivious to what had been going on practically under their noses, it became a common claim among the allies that, 'They must have known!' It is interesting to examine this idea, in light of the experiences of those living during the same period, not in Bavaria or Poland, but only eight miles from the centre of Edinburgh.

Imagine that a number of concentration camps had been set up on the edge of large towns; some only a few miles from major cities. Local farmers heard rumours about atrocities being committed in these places, but when they approached the barbed wire fences, they were warned off by armed guards in watch-towers. Stories circulated about beatings, torture, starvation and even shootings, but so secretive were those running the camps that no solid information ever leaked out. It was also suggested that these sinister locations were being used to hold communists, Jews and homosexuals; although this was never admitted by anybody in authority. If all this sounds as though it could have been the experience of German and Polish civilians during World War Two, at the height of the Holocaust, then it will come as a surprise to learn that the description is actually of various camps set up in the south of Scotland during that same period.

In the House of Commons, on 1 December 1942, Mr Adam McKinlay, the MP for Dunbartonshire in Scotland, rose to ask the Home Secretary how many foreigners were registered with the police on the Isle of Bute. It seemed an innocuous enough question. The island of Bute lies in the Firth of Clyde, about twenty miles west of Glasgow. It is not geographically remote, being served by a regular ferry service and having thousands of inhabitants and all that Mr McKinley apparently wished to know was the number of foreign citizens on the island. The Under-Secretary of State for the Home Office, a Mr Peake, replied that:

The total number is 109, of whom 39 are Belgians, 28 Poles, 15 Italians, eight Dutch, eight Norwegians, six Americans, two Russians, one Brazilian, one Swedish and one German.

At this point, Mr McKinlay pounced. He asked, 'Will the honourable gentleman inform the House on whose instructions a number of Poles are being detained?'

Mr Peake replied that, 'The figures I have given to the honourable member are quite accurate, but if he has any further point to bring to my notice, I should be glad to consider it.'

'I am trying to indicate that there are more than 28 Poles upon the Isle of Bute and to ask on whose instructions they are there and why they are so detained.'

This should have been a sensational exchange, as an MP was accusing a representative of the Home Office of lying to the House. He was also hinting that people were being detained illegally at some location in the British Isles. The response was brief and dismissive, the Under-Secretary saying merely, 'That would not be a question for me to answer.'

It was plain that something was going on regarding Polish people being locked up in part of Scotland and that the MP for a nearby area was keen to find out the details. It was also equally clear that the Home Office, and by implication the government, had no intention of telling the House of Commons what was happening on the Isle of Bute.

This was not the first time that the subject of Polish prisoners in Scotland had been raised in the House of Commons. The previous year, Samuel Silverman, MP for Nelson and Colne, had been concerned about the arrest and imprisonment of two Polish Jews; the brothers Benjamin and Jack Ajzenberg. They had apparently been picked up in London by Polish soldiers and then taken to Scotland and held in a camp there. After some unsatisfactory explanation had been provided, Mr Silverman asked the Secretary for War on 19 February 1941:

How many persons are now detained by the Polish authorities in this country under their powers under the Allied Forces Act; and how many persons are now detained by the Polish authorities who have never at any time served in the Polish armed forces?

The answer was fairly vague, to the effect that apart from soldiers, only six people were currently being held by the Polish authorities under the terms of the Allied Forces Act.

A few years later, shortly after the end of the war in Europe, there was still unease in parliament about the activities of the Polish 'authorities' in Scotland. On 14 June 1945 Robert McIntyre, Member of Parliament for the Scottish constituency of Motherwell, rose in the House of Commons to ask the following question, which is worth quoting in full. He wished to know whether the Under-Secretary of State for Scotland

Will make provision for the inspection, at any time, by representatives of the various districts of Scotland of any penal settlements, concentration camps, detention barracks, prisons, etc. within their area, whether these institutions are under the control of the British, American, French or Polish governments or any other authority; and for the issuing of a public report by those representatives.

The official response to this question managed in the most spectacular way imaginable, to miss the point. Speaking for the government, Mr Chapman said:

My Noble Friend will be glad to arrange for hon. Members to visit at
any time any of the civil prisons or Borstal institutions under his control.
All these establishments already have Visiting Committees consisting of
representatives of local authorities or of other public men and women.
My Noble Friend has no jurisdiction over premises maintained by the
Service authorities or by Allied Governments

It is obvious from looking at these parliamentary exchanges, that
something troubling was taking place in Scotland during the Second
World War and that the government of the day did not wish to see a
fuss being made about the matter. In the last parliamentary question
at which we have looked, specific reference was made to the possible
existence of penal settlements or concentration camps in Scotland and,
once again, the government spokesman simply fails to respond in any
meaningful way. To understand what these camps were and why the
British government should have been prepared to tolerate their existence,
it will be necessary to look in some detail at the history of Poland in the
years between 1918 and 1939 and also in the opening years of World War
Two.

It is sometimes forgotten, when looking at developments in Europe
during the 1930s, that Germany and Italy were not the only dictatorships
at that time. Spain and Poland were also run by men who distrusted and
rejected the very idea of democracy. In 1926 Marshal Josef Pilsudski led
a military coup, seizing control of Poland by armed force. At the head
of a column of soldiers, he marched into parliament and announced to
the startled deputies, 'I shit on you all!'. This action neatly illustrated
Pilsudski's contempt for the democratically elected politicians who were
running the country at that time.

Shortly before Pilsudski's death in 1935, a concentration camp was
opened in an old prison in the west of the country, which is now part of
Belarus. The *Miejsce Odosobniennia w Berezie Kartuskiej*, which translates
as 'Place of isolation at Bereza Kartuska' was established by Pilsudski for
the detention of those whom he viewed as a threat to, 'security, peace
and social order.' Thousands of people were held at Bereza Kartuska,
including journalists, communists and Ukrainian nationalists.

Throughout the 1930s, hand in hand with an increasingly harsh and authoritan government, Poland began to adopt various anti-Semitic measures, similar in many ways to those being enforced in neighbouring Nazi Germany. Jews were being prevented from joining some professions and also discriminated against in the army; an important point to which we shall later return.

Some readers may perhaps be scratching their heads at this point and wondering what all this has to do with the camps being run by Poland on British soil. What were Polish forces doing in Scotland in the first place? The answer to that lies in the events which shook Europe in 1940. After the invasion of Poland by German and Russian forces in the summer of 1939, elements of the Polish army left their own country and regrouped in France. When Germany attacked France the following year, they fought alongside the French. Following the fall of France, many Polish troops found their way to Britain, where they were allowed to form themselves into a new army.

The British reasons for offering shelter to the Polish forces were not wholly altruistic. During the disastrous retreat from France, the evacuation from Dunkirk, the British army had lost huge numbers of men, along with enormous quantities of material; vehicles, artillery and so on. After the Fall of France, there was the very real possibility of a German invasion of Britain. Preparing a defence against such an attack posed great problems for the government in London. It was thought most likely that any seaborne invasion would be launched across the channel; landing on the beaches of Sussex or Kent. This at least was the route taken by previous invaders such as Julius Caesar and William the Conqueror. It would then require only a relatively short strike to the north west to seize the capital.

Although a German landing on the south coast was considered the greatest threat, there were also good historical reasons for bearing in mind another possibility, that forces might be landed much further north, enabling the Germany army to gain a foothold from which they could build up their positions until they were ready to drive south and attack London. It will be recalled that in 1066, while the English leaders were anticipating an invasion from Normandy, in modern day France, a

Norwegian army crossed the North Sea, landed in Yorkshire and captured York. In 1940, it was feared that history might repeat itself, with a fleet of ships sailing from Norway to attack Britain either along the Scottish or north east English coast.

Norway had fallen to the Germans in the spring of 1940 and would have made the perfect springboard for an attack on Scotland. This might have proved catastrophic for Britain, most of whose forces were positioned in south east England; ready to deter any attempted landing on the south coast. Scotland was very vulnerable to attack, because many of the troops which should have been defending the east coast of Scotland, from Aberdeen to Edinburgh, had been captured in the retreat from Dunkirk. For example, 10,000 men of the 51st (Highland) Division had been taken prisoner at St Valery-en-Caux in 1940. This meant that there were scarcely enough soldiers to guard even the coastal areas around the major cities of east Scotland; those which might be most at hazard from an invasion force arriving from Norwegian ports.

The tens of thousands of Polish troops which arrived in Britain after the Fall of France in June 1940 were therefore a valuable resource for the British; battle-hardened soldiers who might assist in the defence of the United Kingdom against a German invasion. Assimilating so many men, hardly any of whom spoke English, into the British army would have been a logistical nightmare. There was, in any case, no time to spend on such an enterprise. These soldiers would have to move north at once and take up positions along the coast. The only way this could be achieved would be if they were to retain their own officers and form themselves into an all-Polish army. This was done and by the end of the summer, something like 20,000 Polish soldiers were stationed in and around Edinburgh; responsible for guarding unprotected sections of the North Sea coast.

The first Polish troops arrived in Scotland on 5 August 1940, at the same time as the signing of the Anglo-Polish Military Agreement. In return for the help of the Polish army, the British government granted them a high degree of autonomy, allowing them to regulate their own forces as they saw fit and also to establish bases which were, to all intents and purposes, to be treated as sovereign Polish territory. A short while later

Parliament passed the Allied Forces Act. This allowed the governments in exile of Belgium, The Netherlands, Norway, Czechoslovakia and Poland to raise independent armed forces which would be stationed on British soil.

This *quid pro quo*, allowing the Polish army to run its own affairs in Scotland without any interference from the British authorities, in exchange for their aid in defending the country against invasion, worked well enough in general. In the long term, the British probably believed that by offering such hospitality, they would ensure that at least some post-war European governments would feel indebted to Britain for her assistance in their time of need. What nobody could have guessed was that the leader of the Polish government in exile, General Wladyslaw Sikorski, had from the very start intended to operate concentration camps in the country which was providing him and his fellow countrymen with refuge.

General Sikorski, although Prime Minister of Poland from 1922 to 1923, had not been in favour with the Pilsudski regime and before the outbreak of war in 1939 had been more or less living in exile in Paris. With the partition of Poland between Germany and the Soviet Union in 1939, his time had come and he was appointed Prime Minister once more; this time of the Polish government in exile. Because he was such a controversial figure, with many political opponents, one of the first steps that Sikorski took was to set up a detention facility for his enemies in the small town of Cerizay in western France.

The camp at Cerizay was a fairly relaxed institution, under the command of Colonel Rumsza; a trusted associate of Sikorski. Those confined there had a good deal of freedom, but were not allowed to leave the area. It was Sikorski's way of keeping his political enemies out of circulation. The reason for such easy-going conditions was that Sikorski had already asked the French government to lease him a prison in which to hold his enemies; a request which had been refused. Cerizay was the best that he could manage when it came to controlling those officers and political opponents of whom he disapproved. When the Polish forces left France and moved to Britain, they brought with them the prisoners from Cerizay. The general was determined that none of these important figures, many of whom had held high posts in the previous Polish government, would be allowed the opportunity of conspiring against his leadership.

To begin with, the detainees from Cerizay were held in the Glasgow Rangers stadium, before a more permanent camp was set up near Rothesay on the Isle of Bute. From the beginning, General Sikorski made no secret of his intentions; at least to his fellow countrymen. The British were at first completely in the dark about his plans. At a meeting of the Polish National Council in London, on 18 July 1940, only weeks after the fall of France and the arrival in Britain of the Polish forces, Sikorski announced bluntly that, 'There is no Polish judiciary. Those who conspire will be sent to a concentration camp.' Since his government and army were now firmly established in the British Isles, this could only be interpreted as a tacit admission that concentration camps were to be set up in Britain. Less than a week after the first Polish soldiers set foot in Scotland, General Marian Kukiel, who had been appointed Commander of Camps and Polish Army Units in Scotland by Sikorski, issued a secret order relating to what he described as, 'An unallocated grouping of officers', who were to be held in a special camp.

The ostensible purpose of the camp which the Polish government in exile set up near Rothesay was to screen their army for possible 'fifth columnists'; men who might betray Poland to the Germans. This might have sounded plausible, until one saw the kind of people who were being held there. General Ludomil Antoni Rayski had, before the beginning of the Second World War been the Commander of the Polish Air Force. He had also served in the British Royal Air Force. After the invasion of Poland, he arrived in France, with many other high-ranking officers. The new Prime Minister, General Sikorski, did not trust Rayski, as he had been too closely associated with the previous regime. When France fell to the Germans, General Rayski accompanied the rest of the Polish army to Britain, where he was promptly arrested and held at the camp at Rothesay.

Nor was Ludomil Rayski the only general held prisoner at Rothesay. Stefan Dab-Biernacki was another prominent Polish officer who had enjoyed a glittering career in the army. He too fell foul of Sikorski and was imprisoned on the Isle of Bute. In all, no fewer than twenty generals of the Polish army were prisoners in the Rothesay camp at different times. It wasn't only army officers whom Sikorski suspected of intriguing against him. Another important prisoner was Marian Zyndram-Koscialkowski, who was Prime Minister of Poland from 1935-1936. He was arrested and taken to Rothesay at the same time as Michael GrazynskI, president of the Polish Scouting Association. The idea that any of these men were secretly German agents was frankly absurd. The true reason that they were taken to the Scottish island was that General Sikorski was getting his revenge upon members of the Pilsudski regime and the government which followed it.

Living conditions at the camp at Rothesay were not in the least harsh. Indeed, the establishment was based around a former holiday camp and the inmates lived in the wooden chalets which a year or two earlier had housed those wishing to spend a week by the seaside. As long as they were kept away from the government in exile and were stuck on the island, with no opportunity to plot against Sikorski; this was enough.

What General Sikorski had in effect undertaken was a purge of all elements in the Polish army in Britain whom he thought might be disloyal to him personally. He had carried out this action on the spurious grounds that it was necessary to screen high-ranking soldiers and politicians for pro-German tendencies. These men formed only one group of those at Rothesay. Stanislaw Kot, who had been entrusted by Sikorski with rooting out those whose loyalty was dubious, also wanted to rid the new Polish army of what were termed, 'persons of improper moral level'. This meant drunks, philanderers, gamblers and homosexuals. Those living near the Polish camp were led to believe that the inmates were either collaborators who were in the pay of the Nazis or libertines whose immoral conduct was ruining the discipline of the army.

At one time, there were as many as 1,500 prisoners at Rothesay. The camp became a little unwieldy and there were problems in keeping purely political prisoners, such as the former governor of Silesia, cooped up with promiscuous homosexuals. The decision was taken to separate the political prisoners from what were termed by the Polish leadership; 'pathological' cases; that is to say the drunks, gamblers and those who were sexually promiscuous. A second and harsher camp was accordingly established on the Scottish mainland at Tighnabruich. This village, which in 2002 was voted, 'the prettiest village in Argyll, Lomand and Stirlingshire', is on the coast, facing the isle of Bute. The commandant of this new camp was Colonel Wladyslaw Spalek.

One of the most famous prisoners on the Isle of Bute was the writer, journalist and biographer of Stalin; Isaac Deutscher. Although born in Poland, Deutscher, a Jew, had emigrated to Britain and made a life for himself in that country before the outbreak of war in 1939. In 1940, following Dunkirk and the Fall of France, he travelled to Scotland to volunteer for the Polish army which was now based there. No sooner had he joined up, than Isaac Deutscher found himself interned at the camp at Rothesay. Being both a Jew and also a communist, he was regarded as a dangerous subversive by senior figures in General Sikorski's government in exile. It must have been a sobering experience for the dedicated idealist. He had abandoned his work in London, gone haring up to Scotland and now found that he was immediately imprisoned.

Rothesay and Tighnabruich were not the only detention facilities set up by the Polish army in Scotland. The regime at Rothesay might have been comparatively easygoing, but there were other camps where inmates were definitely shot; either because they tried to escape or as merely as a result of annoying the guards. These camps were more like the traditional idea of a concentration camp, with barbed wire fences, watchtowers and brutal guards. One such place was established very early on, a few months after the Polish forces arrived in Scotland. It was in open farmland at Kingledoors; a collection of villages on the River Tweed, a short distance from Berwick-upon-Tweed.

The precise purpose of the camp at Kingledoors is open to question. According to the Polish government in exile, it was no more than a military detention barracks of the type used by every army in the world. It was a grim place though and there were rumours among local farmers that men were being beaten and starved there. What is certain is that at least one prisoner was killed by shooting in this camp. On 29 October 1940, a Jewish prisoner called Edward Jakubowsky was shot dead by a guard called Marian Przybylski. It was suggested that the prisoner had spoken insulting words to the guard, which had resulted in him losing his temper. The Field Bishop of the Polish Army, Joseph Gawlina, wrote about this case after the end of the war. An inquiry by the Polish army concluded that no blame attached to Przybylski for this killing, but that he had used his weapon in the execution of his official duty. The British police were not involved in the investigation into the young man's death.

The camp at Kingledoors was later moved to Shinafoot in Auchterarder; between Edinburgh and Perth. It soon had an evil reputation in the new location. As at Rothesay, local people were told that the camp contained men who had collaborated with the Germans; something guaranteed to remove all sympathy for them among the British. If everything was open and above board and the camp was no more than the Polish equivalent of a British 'glasshouse', it is hard to see why such stories should have been put about by the guards. There is no doubt that a number of Polish soldiers who happened to come into contact with the Shinafoot camp were horrified at what they learned.

Stanislaw Strumph-Wojtkiewicz was a press officer with the Polish army and at one time found himself in the neighbourhood of Auchterarder. In his book, *Contrary to the Order,* he wrote of what he saw there. He said that he had seen a camp with barbed wire, watchtowers and, as he put it, 'a whole arsenal of camp tribulations'. Speaking to local residents, he soon heard stories of beatings and starvation at this camp.

Another Polish soldier with no axe to grind was Adam Majewski, a military surgeon. He wrote about an occasion when he had been called upon to treat an inmate of the camp at Auchterarder. He said that two military policemen appeared at his surgery with a young man whose head was shaven and who looked as though he had been systematically mistreated for some time. This man, who was scarcely more than a boy, trembled constantly and appeared to be in terror of his life. After he was alone with his patient, Majewski heard about the abuses at the camp. He learned that the commandant was a brutal man who frequently beat prisoners, even knocking their teeth out. Later, the surgeon spoke to those living near the camp, who were forbidden to approach the barbed wire fence, but had all the same heard many disturbing stories about what went on there. Interestingly, the guards from the camp gave exactly the same explanation about those being held in the place as were given at

Rothesay. They were told that the prisoners at Shinafoot were German spies and saboteurs.

It was the testimony of Polish soldiers, appalled by what they had witnessed which led to General Kukiel, who had overall responsibility for the camps, ordering the closure of Shinafoot in 1942 and the court martial of the commandant, Captain Korkiewicz. He was acquitted of all charges, although the suspicion remained that he was a sadistic bully.

It is time to look at the suggestions which were made during and shortly after the end of the Second World War that the camps that have so far been described were used to hold, in addition to homosexuals; Jews and communists. To understand these allegations it is necessary to look at a little more Polish history.

Mention the invasion of Poland in 1939, the event which triggered Britain's declaration of war, and one thinks invariably of Germany's invasion of that country. It is quite true that the German attack on Poland in September 1939 caused the British government to declare war on Germany, but it is sometimes forgotten that another country also invaded Poland that month from the opposite direction. The Molotov-Ribbentrop Pact, signed in August that year between Nazi Germany and Soviet Russia, led to the dismemberment of Poland. It was only twenty-one years earlier that Poland had become an independent country; until 1918, it had been no more than a province of the Russian Empire. This stab in the back by the Russians, who clearly hoped once more to absorb Poland into their own sphere, aroused even greater anger among many Poles than the invasion by Germany. That this was so and that the Polish government in exile and their army were probably more pro-German than they were pro-Russian, may be seen by looking at the composition of the Polish army which was under the control of the government in exile in London.

The Poles served alongside the British during the war and as German units surrendered or were captured, any soldiers of Polish origin who had been serving with the German army ended up being the responsibility of the Polish army. One might have thought, given the fact that both Poland and Britain were at war with Germany, such turncoats would have been treated with great severity, but this was not at all the case. In fact, they were in most cases simply welcomed into the Polish army. A natural consequence of this was that as the war progressed, the Polish army operating alongside the British, came to have an increasingly large proportion of soldiers who had formerly been in the *Wermacht*; sometimes for years.

The actual figures for former soldiers of the German army serving in the Polish forces towards the end of the Second World War are astonishing. Perhaps the most accurate statistics are those collected by the British War Office. According to them, of the 30,000 men in the Polish 1st Corps, which was based in Britain, 16,200 had formerly been in the German army. In total, according to the War Office, out of 39,000 men in the Polish army; 22,484 had previously been with the Germans. In short, over half the Polish forces in 1945 had been German soldiers in the past. One high-ranking Polish officer spoke later of his amazement when he discovered that every single member of his staff had fought with Rommel in the Afrika Corps.

This sheds some light upon the feelings of Polish Jews about serving in an army, the majority of whose members had been, at least nominally, Nazis. Even the men who had been dragooned unwillingly into the German forces had often picked up some of the prevailing mood of anti-Semitism and hatred of communism which were prevalent in the *Wermacht*. There were stories of Jews being beaten up by men who had only recently been German soldiers and with whom Jews were now expected to share barracks. Even before the war, the Polish army had never been a particularly welcoming environment for Jews; now it was ten times worse. It is no surprise that Polish Jews in this country had no desire to serve alongside anti-Semites who had actually fought for the Nazis.

The men at whose stories we have so far glanced, all have one thing in common. Isaac Deutscher, who volunteered and was at once arrested and interned, Edward Jakubowsky, who was shot dead in one of the camps and the brothers Jack and Benjamin Azjenberg, who were mentioned in parliament for having been arrested by the Polish army and taken to Scotland; all were Jews. So too was another of the men who fell foul of the Polish government in exile shortly after the war ended in 1945.

Before looking at this case, we must note the anxiety being expressed about the situation of Jews in the Polish army by MPs in the House of Commons.

That there was historic and endemic anti-Semitism in the Polish army and that this had increased during the Second World War; nobody really denied. Nor was it merely the case that this prejudice was unofficial and limited to junior members of the Polish armed forces. In today's jargon, it was 'institutionalised'; found throughout the whole of the army, from the very top downwards. To give a fairly minor example of the way in which anti-Semitism permeated the whole of the Polish army, during a debate on the subject in parliament on 16 April 1944, Evelyn Walkden, MP for Doncaster, asked if members were aware that:

> *The Polish Army Command made it a condition that E.N.S.A. should not send a single concert party to the Polish army which included a Jewish artist, and that they insist upon that condition? Has that condition been repudiated or annulled?*

One might have thought that such a question would prove excruciatingly embarrassing to the government. The Entertainments National Service Association, or ENSA for short, provided entertainment for allied forces during the war. A number of famous people performed with ENSA, including Gracie Fields, George Formby, Laurence Olivier and Ralph Richardson. It was now being alleged that the high command of the Polish army refused to have Jews entertaining their troops. The reply to Evelyn Walkden's enquiry was surprising. Nobody bothered to deny that what he suggested was true but, it was said, this was not anti-Semitism as such, but simply that the Polish army preferred to have Polish singers and entertainers. In other words, again using modern expressions, this was simply a matter of cultural sensitivity. The Poles naturally preferred their own music and songs. Nobody pointed out that it was quite possible to be both Polish and also Jewish.

Amid stories of Jews in the Polish army who had been bullied and victimised by men who had served in the German army for years, agreement was reached that a number of Jews could be transferred from the Polish to the British army. Other Jews serving with the Polish army could stand it no longer and deserted. They were tracked down, arrested and then taken to one or other of the Scottish camps. On 5 April 1944, the British Foreign Secretary made a speech in which he said that he would have conversations with the Polish government in exile on the subject of the supposed anti-Semitism in their armed forces.

Tom Driberg, the Member of Parliament for Maldon in Essex, was among the most outspoken on the subject of the treatment of Jews in the Polish army based in Britain. He produced evidence during a debate on 6 April 1944 that many sergeants and other NCOs in the Polish army had not only served in the *Wermacht*, but were also actively engaged in Jew-baiting. A number of Jews serving in the Polish forces had approached him, saying that they were subjected to regular and sustained bullying and harassment for no other reason than that they were Jewish. Driberg said:

Man after man said: Now they say, these bullying N.C.O.s, 'We cannot do anything in this country, because Churchill, as we all know, is in the pay of the Jews; but you wait until we get you on the continent of Europe, in the second front, then every Pole has two bullets- the first for a Jew and the second for a German.'

It was of course NCOs of this type who were in charge at the camps in Scotland to which Jewish deserters were being taken.

There can be no doubt, and no serious effort was made to deny it at the time, that the Polish army was a particularly inhospitable and unattractive place for Jews in the later years of the Second World War. It was also the fact that Jews who were either in the army, or who the Polish government in exile thought *should* be in the army, ended up behind barbed wire in the camps in Scotland. We also know that a number were killed in the camps or while apparently escaping from them. These deaths were not investigated by the British police, who had no jurisdiction in the matter under the provisions of the Allied Forces Act. The Polish army were not even obliged to notify the British when such deaths took place in their camps.

This then was the situation as the war drew to a close. The Polish government in exile were running at least four or five camps in Scotland, where men termed, 'moral deviants' were being held. Some of these men were homosexuals. The camps also contained a high proportion of Jews. From 1945 onwards, communists too began to find themselves liable to arbitrary arrest and detention in one of the camps.

On 14 June 1945, just weeks after the end of the war in Europe, the Russian newspaper *Pravda* carried an extraordinary article, which was later quoted on Moscow radio. It said:

The Polish Fascist concentration camp system, notorious before the Germans started Buchenwald and other camps, was preserved when the Poles fled from Poland. They found a cosy shelter at Inverkeithing, where in the midst of British rules and customs, and surrounded by barbed wire, lies a patch of Fascist Poland. Patriots refusing to serve under the clique headed by Arecisewski, also democratically minded Poles and members of the Polish Workers Party are being ruthlessly treated or killed when attempting to escape.

The British hastened to deny that there was any truth in the story, claiming that the institution referred to in Inverkeithing was no more than an ordinary military barracks run by the Polish army. Once again, the arrest and detention of a Jew was at the back of the problem.

After the war in Europe ended, a communist government was installed in Poland. This was backed by the Soviet Union, who had *de facto* power in the country, since it had been liberated by the Red Army. The Polish government in exile, which was based in London, was thus rendered obsolete and irrelevant. The most that they were able to do was to mount a rearguard action; trying to prevent Poles from returning to their own country and supporting the new regime. Some Poles living in Britain though were left-wingers who were strongly in favour of the new government in Warsaw. One such man was Dr Jan Jagodzinski, a Jewish academic who had served in the Polish army. When the communist government took over Poland, an official Polish news agency was set up.

It was called Polpress and the London representative of the bureau was Dr Jagodzinski.

At one time, Dr Jagodzinski had served in the Polish army and this gave the government in exile the excuse that they needed to put out of action one of the men who was collaborating with the new communist government. The Polish government in exile in London could see that after waiting patiently throughout the war and fighting valiantly n the side of the allies, they were about to be rendered irrelevant by men such as Jagodzinski, whose loyalty lay with the new regime.

On the evening of Friday 8 June 1945, police officers arrived at the Fleet Street office of Polpress and arrested Dr Jagodzinski. They took him to a nearby police station, where he was handed over to Polish military police. These men then promptly spirited the head of Polpress off to Scotland, where he was held in the camp at Inverkeithing. The British Home Office had instructed Scotland Yard and the Metropolitan Police that nobody was to be handed over to the Polish army in this way without their express permission. The Allied Forces Act and also the Anglo-Polish agreement certainly made provision for cooperation between the civil authorities in Britain and the Polish army, but the British government were beginning to feel a little uneasy at the actions of their Polish allies. All else apart, they did not wish for any embarrassing complications with Russia; which is exactly what happened when news of Dr Jagodzinski's arrest leaked out.

What was to turn into an international incident had happened because the Polish military police had approached the City of London Police with the request for assistance. This force is entirely separate from the Metropolitan Police, the area which they cover includes Fleet Street. The Poles, rather ingenuously, represented Jagodzinski's case as being that of a deserter on the run; making no mention at all of the political aspect of the affair. When they got wind of what had happened, the Home Office moved quickly to lean on the Polish army and get them to release Dr Jagodzinski, but the damage had already been done. No sooner was he released, than the Russians began to make their claims about the existence of concentration camps in Scotland.

The idea that they were allowing concentration camps to be run in their own country was not one that the British felt that they could ignore.

It was accordingly arranged that members of the press and various other people should be shown round the camp at Inverkeithing, which was where Jagodzinski had been briefly detained. The aim was a laudable one, but it is open to question how much good this public relations exercise actually did; at least as far as allaying fears that Polish concentration camps were operating on British soil.

On 13 June 1945, a group of reporters, including a representative of the Press Association, was conducted around the camp at Inverkeithing. Based in an old mansion, there were also two huts. At the time of the visit, fifty-three men were being held there. As the reporter from the *Manchester Guardian* wryly remarked, 'There was ample evidence of shortage of accommodation'. One alarming fact which emerged in the course of a conversation with the camp Commandant was that only two weeks earlier, a prisoner had been shot dead at the camp. This death had allegedly occurred during an escape, but there had been no sort of enquiry afterwards. The local police had been informed, but of course under the Allied Forces Act, they had no jurisdiction in the matter. This was not the only disconcerting revelation made during the visit by the press.

The journalists were given permission to speak to some of the prisoners and it was perhaps unfortunate that the first man to whom they spoke happened to be yet another Jew. Josef Dobosiewicz, a 23-year-old soldier who had fought with the Canadian army in Holland and spoke with a Canadian accent, said that he had been held in Inverkeithing for more than two months, accused of stealing a suitcase. He went on to allege that some prisoners were kept chained up in cells; an allegation which caused visible shock among the newspaper reporters, who included several from the United States. It turned out that this was perfectly true and eventually the Commandant sent for the chains and explained that these were also used in the British army for restraining violent and recalcitrant prisoners.

That not everything was as it should be at the camp was by this time obvious to all of those present. In answer to a question, Dobieswicz said that some men were being held at the camp for political reasons, rather than because they had committed any crime. He went on to claim that one of the guards at Inverkeithing was inhuman. Another prisoner suggested that he had been tricked into returning to Britain from France and that as soon as he had landed, he was brought to the camp. Incredibly, he claimed that he had been happier working as a forced labourer for the Germans in Berlin than he was in the Scottish camp.

At the end of the tour, the Commandant made a statement which must rank as something of an understatement. He said, 'I agree that everything is not all right, but the conditions here are abnormally difficult'.

It is unclear just what the original purpose of the base at Inverkeithing might have been, but during the later years of the war, it was surrounded by barbed wire fences and was used as a prison camp. The line that the Polish army hoped to put across to the press was that Inverkeithing was no more than a penal camp for those soldiers found guilty of breaches of military discipline. All armies of course, including the British, have institutions of this kind. In the British army, they are known by the colloquial name of 'The Glasshouse'; after the military detention facility at Aldershot, which had a glazed roof. The difficulty with this, was that Aldershot was not used for academics who had been snatched from their offices for no other reason than that they had years ago served in the army. There was little reason to doubt that the camps run by the Polish army in Scotland were being used to keep imprisoned Polish men who might otherwise have returned to their own country and become supporters of the new regime which had been established there. It is an uncomfortable fact in every case mentioned in parliament or referred to in the newspapers; the prisoners were Jewish.

The British government were caught in a very hard situation after the end of the Second World War. They had backed the Polish government in exile and seen it out-manoeuvred by the Soviets, who installed their own nominees in Poland to form the new government. Short of declaring war on Russia, there was little to be done about this. This left the British lumbered with a government which had no power or influence at all in its own country, but was still maintaining an army on British soil; an army operating in tandem with a network of penal camps of a most dubious nature.

It was hardly possible to ditch an allied government which had been such a loyal supporter of Britain at a critical time when she was fighting for her very survival. Nevertheless, it was, as the months passed, increasingly clear that the Polish government in London was governing little; other than the army which was still based in Scotland. That the government in exile was in no hurry to concede defeat to the new, Moscow-leaning government in Poland, may be seen by the fact that a year after the end of the war in Europe, Jews were still being imprisoned in the camps in Scotland.

On 16 April 1946, Mr William Gallacher, the MP for Fife West, rose in the Commons to ask the Secretary of State for War:

> If he is aware that two Polish Jewish soldiers, David Glicenstein and Shimon Getreuthendler, have been sentenced by Polish court martial to terms of imprisonment; if he will enquire into these cases which represent victimisation of two Jewish soldiers who were among those who left the Polish army owing to anti-Semitic conditions in 1944; if he is aware that they were charged with being absent from their units at a time after the amnesty had been issued on 25 June 1945; and if he will cause the sentences to be rescinded so that these Polish Jewish soldiers can return to their own country as they wish to do.

That there was something pretty unsavoury going on in Scotland during the Second World War and for some time after it, seems certain. Just what it was that was happening is less clear. The Polish army were definitely running camps there; camps which General Sikorski, the leader of the Polish government in exile, referred to as 'concentration camps'. There were also penal institutions where prisoners were mistreated and even killed. Whether these places too were concentration camps or just ordinary, military detention barracks is impossible at this late stage to establish. The Polish army, directed by their government in London, were very keen to claim that anybody whom they wished to lock up was, or had been, a soldier in their army and therefore a person over whom they had legal jurisdiction under the terms of the Allied Services Act.

It is perhaps worth mentioning that if the Polish government in exile was desperately keen to prevent Poles from returning to their own country to work in support of the new, Moscow-backed administration there, then the communists were only too ready to blacken the name of the official government in exile. This was done by using such epithets as 'fascist' and also by referring to the use of 'concentration camps'. That some of these claims were purely propaganda cannot be doubted. Even so, it is exceedingly odd that every single person whose name we now know who was detained in these places was Jewish. Even allowing for the fact that the Soviet Union was milking the situation for any advantage to their own position; it seems inescapably true that the Polish government in exile seemed very ready to lock up Jews in their special camps.

Ultimately, the only safe verdict to deliver on some of the more extreme stories emerging from those times is the old Scottish one of 'Not Proven'. Enormous suspicion attaches itself to the actions of the Polish army in Britain when it came to the detention of their fellow countrymen, but it is not possible to say with any degree of certainty that all the sites at which we have looked were really concentration camps, in the sense that we have been using the expression. We will perhaps have to wait for more evidence to emerge, before we can say for sure what was going on at such places as Inverkeithing and Shinafoot.

Chapter Six

1945-1948
Crimes Against Humanity: Slave Labour
Camps in Post-War Britain

Most people in Britain are familiar with the film, *Bridge on the River Kwai*, which tells the story of British prisoners of war being used as slave labour in a civil engineering project. Tourists from this country go to Thailand and visit the railway line; the construction of which is the central theme of the film. It is not necessary however to go to south-east Asia to see such things. Anybody wishing to visit a transport link which was built by slave labour in the 1940s, need only travel to the London Underground station of Debden, which is on the Central Line. Rectory Lane, shown in Plate 10, is a road which lies only 200 yards from the tube station and it was built by some of the hundreds of thousands of slave labourers who were confined in over 600 camps on the outskirts of most British cities and many large towns in the years following the end of the Second World War.

The very idea of prisoners of war or civilians being used as slave labour strikes most of us as abhorrent and led to those who organised slave labour camps, both in the far East and Europe, being tried after the end of the Second World War for crimes against humanity. The Charter of the International Military Tribunal which was drawn up before the trial of the Nazi leaders at Nuremberg, specifically stated in Article 6 that enslavement was a crime against humanity. In light of this, it is interesting to note that in 1947, two years after the end of the Second World War, 25 per cent of the land workforce in Britain consisted of slave labourers. Despite hanging a number of German war criminals for being involved in the running of slave labour camps, slave labour was an integral part of the British economy and camps holding these workers were scattered throughout the country; camps which contained hundreds of thousands of men being used as forced labour. On building sites and farms, in factories and on roads, these slave labourers helped to forge Britain's post-war prosperity.

The Second World War ended in Europe on 7 May 1945, with the unconditional surrender of all German armed forces. Throughout the conflict, the British had been extremely punctilious about the necessity for all parties to abide by the various provisions of the 1929 Geneva Convention on the rules of war. These concerned, among other things, the correct treatment of prisoners of war. Prisoners should receive sufficient food, adequate medical care and must be removed from areas of conflict as soon as possible after their capture. Article 75 of the Geneva Convention dealt with the release and repatriation of prisoners of war. This was to take place with the least possible delay after the conclusion of peace.

For a nation which had for six years been so concerned about strict adherence to the letter and spirit of the Geneva Convention, one might have supposed that the situation was very clear. The war with Germany had ended in May 1945 and the British and their allies had a duty to repatriate all prisoners of war to their home countries as soon as possible. We shall look briefly at how the other allied nations abided or failed to abide by this particular article of the Geneva Convention in a little while, but for now we must note that the British had at the end of the war something approaching half a million German, Italian and other prisoners of war whom they were morally obliged to return to their own countries as swiftly as possible. In fact, far from sending the prisoners home, the British government began to transport as many as possible, from across the world, to the British Isles. Many German POWs were being held, on behalf of Britain, in Canada and the United States and these too were sent not to Germany or Italy, but to camps in Britain. It soon became apparent that the British government, for reasons of their own, had no intention at all of obeying Article 75 of the 1929 Geneva Convention and repatriating prisoners of war.

Before exploring in detail what happened to these men after the end of the war, perhaps we should see how the allies managed to ride a coach and horses through the Geneva Convention in this way; after having been so vociferous in their appeals for other countries to acknowledge and comply with their own duties in that regard. Two stunning pieces of sophistry were used to justify this flagrant breach of the principles of the Geneva Convention and even to this day, few people know how such a piece of sharp practice was undertaken.

The first trick used not only by the British, but also by other allied nations was to pretend that the war was not really over at all and that there was therefore no obligation to send prisoners of war home. This was very neatly accomplished by pointing out that the German surrender had been unconditional and that no armistice had consequently been signed. There are various ways of bringing a war to an end. The commonest is by means of an armistice. This is a legal agreement by various sides in a conflict that they will stop fighting at a certain time and usually sets out what will then happen. The First World War was of course ended by such an agreement; which is why we celebrate 11 November, the anniversary of the signing of the document, as Armistice Day and the nearest Sunday as being Remembrance Sunday. The 1918 armistice laid out arrangements for ending the fighting and bringing the war to an end. Provisions were made for the return of prisoners of war to their own countries.

In the case of an unconditional surrender, no guarantees are given to a defeated enemy about what will happen next. Everything which follows such a surrender is dependent upon the good will of the victor or victors. Because the Second World War was brought to an effective end by this means, the allies gave no promises or undertakings at all regarding the eventual fate of any prisoners in their hands. Surprisingly, the formal end of the Second World War and the final arrangement of all outstanding matters was not legally agreed until 1990! Under the terms of the *Treaty on the Final Settlement with Respect to Germany*, Germany finally became a sovereign nation with control over all parts of the country, including Berlin, on 15 March 1991.

Of course, this ignoring of the glaring fact that the war was over and using it as an excuse to retain prisoners, was seen by many as a rather shabby trick and flagrant violation of the principles of the Geneva Convention. A second, and even craftier device was resorted to. The Geneva

Convention requires prisoners of war to be fed at a similar level to the troops of those who have captured them. They must also be housed in certain conditions and given access to religious services, sports facilities and so on. As the war drew to a close and the number of prisoners held by the allies rose to the tens of millions, it simply was not possible to house and feed them all to the same standards as soldiers in the British and American armies. Since many of these prisoners had not actually been captured during fighting, but had rather fallen into allied hands as the war ended, the decision was taken by both the Americans and British that they would not treat or even classify these enemy troops as prisoners of war. Instead, they would, by the Americans, be designated 'Disarmed Enemy Forces' and by the British, 'Surrendered Enemy Personnel'. This meant that the vast majority of the men held by the allies were no longer technically prisoners of war and accordingly received no protection under the Geneva Convention.

Strictly speaking, the British were perfectly correct in refusing to classify enemy soldiers who had surrendered in vast numbers as the war came to an end, as prisoners of war. According to the 1929 Geneva Convention, a prisoner of war was an enemy combatant who had been *captured*. Those who surrender do not fall into this category.

Having deprived the millions of German soldiers under their control of POW status, mean that they were also no longer entitled to the protection of the Red Cross and that Switzerland, as the 'Protecting Power', could also be denied access to them. Considering the fact that many of them were starving, this was perhaps just as well.

During the later stages of the war, the allies had already made provisional plans to use the forced labour of German prisoners as a form of reparation for the war. The matter was discussed at the Yalta and Potsdam conferences and Winston Churchill was in favour of the idea. The only difficulties were the purely legal ones of how prisoners of war could be used in this way for what amounted in all but name to slave labour. The failure to sign an armistice and the changed status of the prisoners held by the allies meant that they were no longer afforded the protection of the Geneva Convention and that the allied nations could deal with these men as they saw fit.

One point must be disposed of before going any further and that is this. The 400,000 or so prisoners of war in Britain were not beaten, starved or worked to death in the way that those being held in German concentration camps had been. It is true that the accommodation in which they were held would have been in violation of the Geneva Convention, had the British not found such an ingenious way of circumventing this. For instance, because so many had been brought to Britain from America and Canada, there were not enough huts in existing prison camps for them to stay. As a result, during the sharp winter of 1945, many were housed in tents.

By and large though, the conditions under which the hundreds of thousands of prisoners were held were reasonable enough for the period. Their lives were Spartan, but they were not subjected to cruelty or abuse. It remained the fact though that they *were* prisoners and prisoners moreover who were expected to work for their masters; with no prospect of returning home for years, even though the war in which they had been taken prisoner had now ended. It is this which makes it necessary to refer to them as 'slave labourers', rather than the conditions under which they were being kept.

The question of whether slavery can be taking place even when the victims are being well fed and comfortably housed was raised and comprehensively dismissed during one of the Nuremberg trials held in the years following the end of the Second World War. Ironically, these trials of Nazis for enslavement, some of which ended in the hanging of those convicted, took place at the very time that Britain was keeping over a quarter of a million men in slavery. From 8 April to 3 November 1947, for example, the so-called WVHA trial was held in Nuremberg. SS Lieutenant-General Oswald Pohl, along with seventeen other members of the WVHA; the Economic and Administrative Office of the SS. This department was responsible for the many slave labourers held in concentration camps and used in the factories and mines of the Third Reich. Part of the defence of these men was based upon the supposed fact that the slave workers received rations of the same quality as those given to free workers and soldiers and that their living conditions were no worse than those of many German citizens.

The WVHA trial was presided over by Judge Robert Toms of the Circuit Court of Michigan. After seven months of the most painstaking and patient investigation into the whole subject of slavery during the recent war, the tribunal gave their judgement, which read in part:

> *Under the spell of National Socialism, these defendants today are only mildly conscious of any guilt in the kidnapping and enslavement of millions of civilians. The concept that slavery is criminal per se does not enter into their thinking. Their attitude may be summarised thus:*
>
>> *'We fed and clothed and housed these prisoners as best we could. If they were hungry and cold, so were the Germans. If they had to work long hours under trying conditions, so did the Germans. What is wrong with that?'*

The Nuremberg tribunal was not at all impressed by such arguments and went on to declare:

> *Slavery may exist even without torture. Slaves may be well fed and well clothed and comfortably housed, but they are still slaves if without lawful process they are deprived of their freedom by forceful restraint. We might eliminate all proof of ill treatment, overlook the starvation and beatings and other barbarous acts, but the admitted fact of slavery – compulsory uncompensated labour- would still remain. There is no such thing as benevolent slavery. Involuntary servitude, even tempered by humane treatment, is still slavery.*

We must recall at this point that at the very time that this judgement was being given, 25 per cent of the land force in Britain consisted of German prisoners who were being held in defiance of international law and used as forced labour.

Lieutenant-General Pohl and three of his fellow defendants were sentenced to death and hanged. Others received long terms of imprisonment. As the court made clear, the very fact of slavery was held to be a crime against humanity; deserving of the most condign punishment.

Having looked briefly at what it was that the British were doing in the years immediately following the end of the war, and having seen that by all standards, both moral and legal, that it amounted to slavery; let us see in detail what was being done and why.

One of the most surprising aspects of the prisoners of war being held in Britain after the end of the Second World War is that their number went on rising and was still going up a year after the war had ended. At the end of May 1946, there were 373,000 German prisoners in the country. A month later, this had risen to 385,000. The government was ambivalent, one might even say shifty, about the whole business. On the one hand, it was claimed that these men were not *bona fide* prisoners of war and that the Geneva Convention did not therefore apply to them. In the next breath, assurances were given that they were being treated in accordance with the Geneva Convention. In July 1946 Lord Nathan, speaking in the House of Lords on behalf of the government, said:

Far from the Government having set its face against repatriation, there is already a measure of repatriation proceeding and it would be wrong to think that repatriation would be brought to a sudden end.

Yet even as Lord Nathan made this statement, the numbers of German prisoners being held at camps in Britain continued inexorably to rise. What this spokesman for the government had failed to make clear was that the 'measure of repatriation' which was taking place concerned Italian prisoners, rather than Germans. An informal decision had been made that Britain would release Italians, while hanging on for another few years to the German prisoners. Although never made explicit, this was almost certainly because the British regarded the Germans as being infinitely more culpable in precipitating the war than were the Italians. There was also the indisputable fact that all the damage inflicted on the nation by means of bombing raids and missile attacks by V1s and V2s, had been solely caused by Germany.

There were those who thought that the whole thing was deliberately planned by the government for purely economic reasons. For one thing, the prisoners were a profitable enterprise. They were paid a nominal

DISORDER AT LANCASTER CONCENTRATION CAMP.

Newspaper headline from the Manchester Guardian, *of 4 December 1914.*
Manchester Guardian

A French cartoon, drawing attention to the high mortality rates in British concentration camps. Author's collection

Lizzie Van Zuyl, a seven-year-old girl who died of typhoid in a British concentration camp. Author's collection

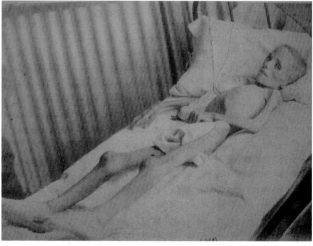

Springfontein Concentration Camp; over 500 hundred women and children died of hunger and disease here. Author's collection

Lord Kitchener, architect of the South African concentration camps. Author's collection

Frongoch Concentration Camp;
it housed thousands of political
prisoners in 1916. Author's
collection

CONCENTRATION CAMPS
FOR THE WORKLESS!!!

Capitalism's Cure
for Unemployment:

SLAVERY!   MILITARISATION!

On behalf of the National Government, Sir John
Gilmour has stated officially that the training camps, to
be established under the new UNEMPLOYMENT BILL,
are "CONCENTRATION CAMPS." CONCENTRATION

A leaflet denouncing the labour camps
operating in Britain during the 1930s.
Author's collection

General Sikorski; the man responsible
for the concentration camps in Scotland.
Author's collection

Rothesay on the Isle of Bute; the first Polish concentration camp was established here in 1940. Author's collection

Rectory Lane - an unremarkable road on the outskirts of London. It was built after the Second World War by slave labourers. Author's collection

Cultybraggen camp - the ubiquitous Nissen huts housed slave labourers between 1945 and 1948. Author's collection

Atlit Camp in British-occupied Palestine. 'Illegal' immigrants were detained here during the late 1940s. Author's collection

One of the concentration camps in Cyprus which held Jews rounded up by the British army. Author's collection

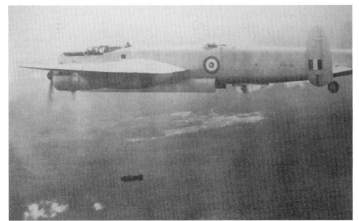

Winning 'hearts and minds'; a bomber of the Royal Australian Air Force pounds the Malayan jungle. Author's collection

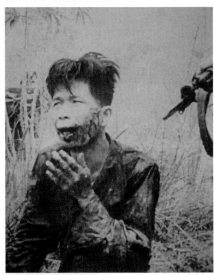

The interrogation of a Chinese guerrilla captured during the Malayan Emergency. Author's collection

British soldiers questioning a civilian in Malaya. Author's collection

British troops hunting for Mau Mau fighters in Kenya. Author's collection

The former RAF base of Long Kesh, while it was being used as Britain's last concentration camp. Author's collection

Long Kesh today. Author's collection

HMS Maidstone, *the Second World War warship used to hold political prisoners in the 1970s.* Author's collection

shilling a day for their work, but even taking this into account and also the costs of housing, feeding and guarding them, the government was still making a profit of £750,000 a week. At a time when rationing was still in force and the British economy not in very good shape, an extra £40 million a year for the Treasury came in very handy.

Then there was the simple fact that there was not enough manpower in the United Kingdom for some purposes. Take agriculture, for instance. Writing in the *Observer* on 11 August 1946, F.W. Bateson made a number of trenchant points about the reliance that was currently being placed upon German labour. Bateson explained that since the outbreak of war in 1939, harvests had been gathered in with the help of the Women's Land Army, conscientious objectors and volunteers from the cities. Now that the war had ended, there was a shortfall in the unskilled labourers needed during the harvest months of August and September. Attempts had been made to fill this gap in much-needed manpower by arranging harvest camps for schoolchildren to come and camp out at farms and help with the harvest, but there were still not enough hands available.

In his article, Bateson explained that between 1929 and 1938, around 1.5 million acres of wheat were cultivated in Britain. Now, with a greatly reduced workforce, 3 million acres were under cultivation. It would be simply impossible to harvest all this wheat without the labour of the German prisoners. But then again, as he also pointed out, the situation would be just the same in 1948. British agriculture had come to rely upon what Bateson charitably described as, 'semi-slave labour'.

This then was one powerful motive for retaining the hundreds of thousands of prisoners being held in Britain. There were 600,000 farm workers in the country and 160,000 prisoners also engaged in farm work. In short, a little over 20 per cent of the agricultural workforce were prisoners.

None of this was ever openly admitted by those who should have been responsible for repatriating the prisoners to Germany. Instead, they hummed and hawed, prevaricated and procrastinated and, as the years passed, the British economy was still benefiting from the forced labour of over a quarter of a million men who were being held, as some argued, illegally.

In all, from 1939 to 1948, there were 1,026 prisoner of war camps in the United Kingdom. Not all were open at the same time though and some were used for more than one purpose. It is impossible to say exactly how many camps remained open after 1945 to accommodate the forced labour workforce upon which the British economy was so dependent. There were certainly over 600 camps still operating in the post-war years.

For the first half of the war, there were far fewer camps in Britain for captured prisoners. There were sound reasons for this. In 1940, when Britain stood alone against the Nazis and an invasion of the country was a very real possibility, it would have been sheer madness to build up large numbers of German prisoners in camps. These could have been freed by paratroops and provided another fighting force for the Germans in the event of an invasion. For this reason, prisoners of war taken in the early years of the Second World War were usually sent by ship to the United States and Canada. When the war ended in 1945, there were hundreds of thousands such prisoners being held on Britain's behalf on the other side of the Atlantic. It was not until the defeat of the Germans in North Africa that large numbers of prisoners of war began to be confined in Britain itself.

The camps in which prisoners were held varied greatly from town to town and city to city. Some were disused factories which had been surrounded with barbed wire, while others consisted of rows of corrugated-iron huts; the type known as Nissen huts. Prisoners were given the same rations as British servicemen and, under the terms of the Geneva Convention, could not be forced to work. Some chose to do so, to ameliorate the boredom of being cooped up in huts all day long.

With the end of the war came two realisations. The first was that parts of Britain were in ruins and that there was likely to be a shortage of labourers ready to repair the bomb damage and also harvest the wheat and build new roads. Hot on the heels of this first realisation came the second; that over 400,000 men were being held in Canada and the USA and needed only to be shipped over to Britain, kept under guard and compelled to work.

We looked earlier in this chapter at the neat little piece of sophistry which enabled the British authorities to strip the prisoners of war of their legal protection and ensure that they could be held indefinitely and made to do whatever was most useful to the victorious country. Even at the time, there were those who knew very well that what was being carried out was immoral, illegal and appallingly hypocritical. Questions were asked in parliament about the plight of the men; some of whom had not seen their families for five years and were desperate to return to their own country. On 27 March 1946, almost a year after the war in Europe had ended, Richard Stokes, the MP for Ipswich, said in the House:

The subject I wish to raise is the treatment, and particularly the continued detention, of prisoners of war captured from the enemy, whoever that enemy may have been, during the recent hostilities. It concerns a very considerable number of men. We were told recently at Question time that there are in this country some 225,00 Germans and about 115,000 Italian prisoners of war, of whom some 267,000 have been put to work ... I think that a great deal of the trial now going on at Nuremberg is completely bogus, and it becomes even more bogus when you consider some of the things which the allied governments are doing at present. They are doing some of those very things for which we are trying the war criminals at Nuremberg, such as forcible detention and slave labour-because it is nothing else when German nationals are detained as they are here.

Interestingly, no real effort was made by anybody in the government to deny any of this. Perhaps they assumed, probably correctly, that there would be little sympathy in Britain for former German soldiers. Many people probably thought that it was only just and right for Germany to make some form of reparation to this country for the damage which had been inflicted during the war and if that meant ignoring the rights of a few Germans, then this was of little concern.

Mr Stokes continued:

I asked the Foreign Secretary on 13 March whether he could give us an assurance that prisoners of war in British hands were being treated in accordance with the terms of the Geneva Convention. He said that the

Geneva Convention did not any longer apply and that the protective Power has been withdrawn.

This ought really to have been sensational news; that the hundreds of thousands of men now being held had no legal protection and that essentially, the British could dispose of them as they saw fit. Despite these shocking revelations, it was to be another two and a half years before the last of these unfortunate men would be allowed to return to their families and homes.

It has to be said that the British were not, by a long chalk, the worst offenders as far as the exploitation of German prisoners in the years following the end of the Second World War was concerned. The Russians had far more prisoners and kept them for a lot longer. The last repatriations of German prisoners from the Soviet Union took place as late as 1956, eleven years after the war had ended. The work which the prisoners were required to undertake in Britain was not especially arduous and nor was it risky. Both the French and Norwegians forced German prisoners to clear landmines, resulting in 275 prisoners being killed in Norway and another 392 badly injured. Norway rejected protests about this, on the grounds that the men were not prisoners of war at all, but rather disarmed forces; precisely the same excuse that the British were using. In France, the situation was even worse. The authorities there estimated in September 1945 that 2,000 German prisoners a month were being killed or maimed carrying out the clearance of land mines.

A typical prisoner of war camp in Britain, where the forced labourers were held, was to be found at a site at which we looked in an earlier chapter: Carpenter's Road in Stratford. This was the location of course, during the First World War, of a concentration camp for interned civilians. During the Second World War and for some years afterwards, it was used to house prisoners of war.

At its height, long after the war had ended, Carpenter's Road held up to 1,500 prisoners in wooden and corrugated-iron huts. It was at this time designated 'Camp 30' held, among others, U-Boat crews, members of Rommel's Afrika Corps and a number of SS men. The camp was swollen after the end of the war with prisoners of war brought back to Britain from Canada and America.

The men being held at Camp 30 went out each day, either to work on farms in Essex or to clear rubble from bombsites and work on rebuilding projects. In retrospect, it is quite plain that the main purpose in holding such large numbers of men was to use their labour to help the country recover from the ravages of war, but this was sometimes concealed and a more noble motive put forward. This was that the Germans were only being held so that they could be instructed in the ways of democracy and to make sure that they did not return to Germany and at once start working towards a Fourth Reich! Between 1945 and 1948, civil servants from the Foreign Office made regular visits to Camp 30 so that they could assess the morale of the men held there and the extent to which they had absorbed British values and could therefore be safely allowed to go back to their own country. In the meantime, of course, it made sense that the men carried out hard labour to atone for their previous, misguided beliefs.

The prisoners themselves were not taken in by all this and knew very well that the real purpose of holding them was so that their energy could be devoted to repairing the war damage in Britain, rather than helping rebuild their own shattered country. One of the inspectors from the Foreign Office noted in August 1947:

In one quarter, the view was expressed that the latest emergency measures taken by the British government to secure maximum output in England smack somewhat of totalitarianism.

This was a devastatingly accurate judgement on the methods being used by the British at that time to maintain their economy by means of forced labour. Of course, until the men being held had repented of their sins and admitted the error of their ways, it would hardly be safe to free them, especially when some of them were evidently intent on going straight back to Germany and getting up to all sorts of terrorist activities. According to one report by the Foreign Office, there were plans by some Nazi prisoners to begin a sabotage campaign in Germany and form a resistance movement to fight the occupying allied armies.

Fostering the illusion that the aim of holding so many prisoners for such a long time was really for their own good, some kind of 'denazification' programme, of course gave the British the perfect excuse to hang on to this free labour force for as long as was humanly possible. After they had finished working, contacts were encouraged between the Germans and the people of East End. They were taken to meet local councillors, they played football and attended social events in the area surrounding the camp. They may have been, certainly were in fact, slave labourers, but it was slavery of the most benevolent kind.

By 1948, it was becoming impossible to maintain the pretence any longer that these men were being held for re-education and so they were finally allowed to go back to their own country. The final report on the men being held at Camp 30 said that:

With a few exceptions these men will return to Germany balanced in outlook and in the fullest realisation that a Third World War between Britain and Germany is unthinkable. The most important factor in their re-education has been the excellent civilian contacts and this in spite of the fact that the majority of the men have been stationed in the heart of the East End of London.

This official version of the use of hundreds of thousands of slave labourers over a period of more than three years might perhaps have assuaged the consciences of those in government, but there is no reason to suppose that anybody else was deceived as to the true nature and purpose of keeping the men here until 1948, and even in some cases 1949. Certainly the Prime Minister of Britain, Clement Atlee, had no doubts at all about the reason for detaining so many prisoners and it had little to do with rehabilitating former Nazis and schooling them in the finer points of democracy. On 27 August 1947 Clement Atlee wrote to Victor Gollancz, the publisher, and also Chairman of the Save Europe Now organisation. His letter was in reply to a memorial which had been sent to him, drawing attention to the plight of the German prisoners and signed by 2,000 important figures. Bearing in mind that this was two and a half years after the end of the war in Europe; the Prime Minister's response is chilling in its casual attitude to the hundreds of thousands of men still being held in this country. He said:

> *I sympathise with the human considerations which are put forward in the memorial, but I cannot share the view that the retention of German prisoners of war in foreign countries for labour purposes is inequitable... I need not emphasise the importance of the work being carried out by German prisoners of war in the United Kingdom, particularly in agriculture... We are satisfied that the material conditions in which the prisoners of war work in this country... are entirely adequate and that all reasonable freedom and amenities are available... I scarcely think that it would serve any practical purpose to try to secure international agreement on the completion of repatriation by a date earlier than the end of 1948. I cannot make any promises at this stage and it would be wrong to give the prisoners the impression that they could hope for a change in our present programme, particularly now that our need for agricultural man-power has so greatly increased ...*

There is something monstrously cold-blooded about the above letter. Atlee talks about 'all reasonable freedom' being available, but of course these were men who were being held in Nissen huts, behind barbed-wire fences; guarded by the army. How much freedom did they really have? The talk of 'adequate material circumstances' sounds quite humane, until we recall that this was exactly the line adopted by defendants at the Nuremberg trials; that the slave labourers were housed well and had enough to eat. Some of those responsible for slave labour in Germany and occupied countries during the war, were hanged for this same crime, justified by exactly the same excuses, after being tried for crimes against humanity.

So what were conditions like for the Germans who were still being held, years after the war had ended? They were probably roughly comparable to those of the soldiers guarding them. It is true that when so many prisoners were first brought back from Canada and the United States, some were housed for a while in tents; which was not really acceptable during the winter, but after the initial chaos, all those being used for forced labour were housed in the same sort of huts that British soldiers used themselves. In fact the prison camps looked like ordinary barracks; the only difference being that those living in the camps were not free to come and go as they pleased. They were kept warm, fed as decently as anybody else in post-war Britain and not physically mistreated. The brutal fact remained though, that they were slaves.

A number of these camps are still standing and looking at them from the comfortable perspective of the twenty-first century, it has to be said that they look pretty grim. Eden Camp in North Yorkshire consists of single-story, brick barrack-rooms with asbestos roofs. Today, Eden Camp is a war museum, but the layout of the camp is still clear. Interestingly, the guards' quarters are identical to the prisoners quarters. In other words, the standard of life and lifestyle for both guards and prisoners was pretty much the same; with one great difference. That difference is symbolised by the watchtower on the edge of the buildings. The army guards were of course able to walk out of the gate whenever they felt like it; the prisoners were not. They were counted twice a day and their movements closely regulated.

Another of the camps which is still standing is Cultybraggan in Scotland. This is shown, as it is today, in Plate 11. This was a high-security establishment, which held many members of the SS. The accommodation at Cultybraggan was in Nissen huts and from the air, it looks like what it was; a concentration camp. This camp was, like some of those which we looked at in an earlier chapter, guarded by Polish troops. Five prisoners from this camp were executed for a murder committed at Cultybraggan; the lynching of a supposed informer.

What is rather curious is the way in which the propaganda reasons given by some at the time, and not the genuine purpose in keeping so many men and preventing them from returning to their own countries have been remembered today and adopted as the official version of events. The reality was that Britain was desperately short of agricultural manpower in the first few years after the end of the Second World War and preventing prisoners from leaving the country made perfect sense from a purely economic viewpoint. This was understood to be the case and openly admitted, even by the Prime Minister himself. The legend has grown up though, that the real motive in hanging on to the German prisoners of war was an idealistic one; to re-educate them and inculcate them with the British sense of fair play and love of democracy.

Speaking in 2010, apropos of confidential documents unearthed at The National Archives, detailing the denazification of prisoners held in East London, one historian at least swallowed the official alternative history unquestioningly. Of the prisoners who were held until 1948, those working the land, Nick Hewitt from the Imperial War Museum said, 'It is a reasonable supposition that those prisoners retained for a long period after the war were considered high-risk.' That is to say that according to this historian, the purpose of keeping all those men was not, as Clement Atlee admitted, because they were useful farm labourers, but because they were at risk of carrying back to Germany, incorrect political views and opinions.

There was increasing pressure on the government in many quarters to release the prisoners being held in Britain. Despite the fact that it was hoped to keep them locked up in Britain and available for the 1948 harvest in the autumn, there was such unease about the whole enterprise that it was decided to free them earlier than had originally been planned. In his letter to Save Europe Now, the Prime Minister had hinted that there was no question of sending the Germans home before the end of 1948, but such was the opposition to this, that the government was forced to bring forward the date of the repatriations.

On 13 July 1948, the Secretary of State for War, Emmanuel Shinwell, announced in Parliament that the repatriation of German prisoners of war had been completed the previous day, with the exception of a small number of invalids and others. It had taken over three years, but Britain's experiment with slave labour had come to an end.

It is curious that this episode in British history has vanished almost without trace. Although at the time newspapers and questions being asked in parliament made extensive reference to 'slave labour'; this has been quite forgotten today. That Germans were building roads in some district or other may be vaguely remembered to this day, but even the oldest inhabitants, who recall those days, make no mention of forced labour or slavery. It is almost as though there is a refusal to acknowledge that such a thing could ever have happened in this country.

Chapter Seven

1946-1949
Locking up Holocaust Survivors: The
Concentration Camps of Cyprus

The images of Belsen which were seen after the camp's liberation in 1945, shocked the whole world when they were show on cinema newsreels. That such a place could have existed in the twentieth century seemed utterly grotesque to many people in Britain. Once the survivors of this hell on earth were freed, they would surely be treated with understanding and compassion by all those who knew what they had endured? One might indeed have thought so, but one would have been quite mistaken. There was one nation in the world which would not only lock those survivors up again in concentration camps, once they had been liberated from Belsen, but was also prepared to ship them back to the very country where they had suffered such terrible privations and hold them there; even when they had fled half-way around the world to escape the memory of their captivity in the notorious concentration camps of the Nazi regime. The country which felt able to behave in such a way was of course Britain and the story of how survivors of the Holocaust were, once again, confined in squalid conditions behind barbed wire fences is a horrible one.

After the end of the Second World War, many Jews felt that they had no future anywhere in Europe. They wished to leave the scene of so many atrocities and massacres behind them and make new lives for themselves somewhere quite new. Some travelled to the United States and others to South America. For many though, the logical place of refuge was the historical land of Israel, which was currently being administered by the British, under a mandate granted by the now defunct League of Nations. The British were playing their usual, colonial game of divide and rule in the area which was known at that time as Palestine. Having helped set the Jews and Arabs at each others throats, so preventing them from making common cause against the British army of occupation, they were now struggling desperately to maintain some sort of order in the Holy Land. One way in which this was being done was by restricting immigration into the country; immigration driven largely by the many Jews who were fleeing the wreckage of post-war Europe. Having contributed to the death toll of the Holocaust by limiting the number of Jews entering their territory after the Nazis came to power in 1933, the British were now determined to prevent the survivors of the worst disaster ever to befall the Jewish people from seeking refuge in their ancestral homeland.

The opening passage of the film *Exodus*, which starred Paul Newman, is set in Cyprus. An American woman is asking a Cypriot guide what all the fuss is at the harbour. He tells her, 'Prison ship has arrived, full of Jews for the camps, madam.' When she asks what camps he is referring to, he tells her:

Detention camps out at Karaolos. You see the Jews, they charter a ship from Europe to get to Palestine. Then the British catch the ship and send the whole bunch here.

This brief exchange sums the matter up in a nutshell. Jews were leaving Europe and trying to enter Palestine. The British conceived it to be their duty to prevent them from getting anywhere near their destination and when they caught them, the British army took them prisoner and locked them up in camps on Cyprus. Later on, some were then deported to Europe and, incredible to relate, even sent back to Germany; part of which the British were now running.

What were the camps of Cyprus like? In 1947 Golda Meir, who would go on to become Prime Minister of Israel in later years, visited Cyprus to see for herself what the conditions were like in the camps. She wrote:

They looked like prison camps, ugly clusters of huts and tents – with a watchtower at each end – set down on the sand, with nothing green

or growing anywhere in sight. There wasn't nearly enough water for
drinking and even less for bathing despite the heat.

Plate 13 shows one of the camps in Cyprus. That only two years after the
end of the Holocaust, the British should think it a good idea to confine
Jews to camps of this sort is bad enough, but there was worse. Because
they believed that the situation in Palestine was likely to deteriorate if any
more Jews landed in the country, the British tried to stop them leaving
Europe at all. Almost unbelievably, one of the places where they kept Jews
locked up in Europe was that most iconic of concentration camps, Belsen.

After the end of the Second World War in 1945, the British continued
to run Belsen as a displaced persons' camp. They tried to rename it, to
avoid the awful associations of the name, calling it the Hohne Camp.
Nobody though, least of all those living there, ever knew it as anything
other than Belsen. Many of the Jews remaining in the camp wished to go
to Palestine, which the British were determined to prevent. Friction grew
in the months following the defeat of Germany and the British military
authorities grew impatient with the residents of the displaced persons
camp. It was said that some were involved in black-market dealings, while
others were leaving the camp to try and travel, illegally as the British
saw it, to Palestine. Whatever the truth of the matter, there is no doubt
at all about the step taken by the British army at the end of May 1946.
Here is the text of an announcement by the military officer in charge
of Belsen at that time. The camp is referred to by the preferred British
name of Hohne:

In the last week numerous crimes have been found to have been committed
by persons residing in Hohne Camp. Repeated warnings have been given
that such lawlessness must cease. Repeated requests have been made to
the law-abiding majority in the camp to expose the lawless elements
living amongst them to the military. It is considered that inhabitants
are equally responsible for instigating or allowing these crimes.

Since both warnings and requests have gone unheeded the Military
Commander has decided to confine all inhabitants of Hohne camp to
the area of the camp until further notice. No displaced person will be

permitted to leave the camp without written authority of U.N.R.R.A.
Anyone found outside the confines of the camp without such written
authority will be immediately imprisoned.

Following this announcement, inmates of the camp tried to leave and
were prevented from doing so by British troops. At one point, a fire-hose
was turned on them. It was a peculiarly unedifying sight; British soldiers
using violence to prevent Jews from escaping from Belsen Concentration
Camp.

According to the British, the 'lawlessness' alluded to in the statement
entailed black-market racketeering, but there was another reason that it
was felt wise to prevent Jews leaving the camp and that was because
many of them had as their ultimate aim emigration from Europe to the
Middle East. In fairness to the British, it must be pointed out that they
were not the only nation reopening Nazi concentration camps and using
them for their own purposes. Precisely the same thing was happening
in the Russian zone of Germany.

Well into the 1950s, Buchenwald Concentration camp was still going
strong, having been renamed NKVD Soviet Special Camp No 2. Similarly,
Sachsenhausen was now known as NKVD Soviet Special Camp No 7.
The NKVD was an earlier incarnation of the KGB and they used the
camps to detain political enemies of the new East German regime.

It might be wise to pause at this point and see how the British managed
to get themselves into such a strange situation, so soon after the end of
the Holocaust. When Belsen was liberated by British forces in 1945, who
could possibly have guessed that in little over a year, the British army
would themselves be keeping Jews locked up in the former concentration
camp?

Even before the First World War had ended, the Great Powers had
begun to divide up the territory of their enemies; the British and French
being particularly keen on gaining a foothold in the Middle East. This
had to be done, while at the same time assuring the Arab tribes of the
Ottoman Empire that they would have their own autonomous kingdom
once the Turks had been driven out of Arabia. The French gained
Syria and Lebanon, while the British managed to acquire Palestine and

Mesopotamia; modern day Iraq, Jordan and Israel. Mesopotamia was valuable because it included the Mosel oil fields.

At the same time that they were intriguing for territory of their own, while still satisfying the demands of Arab nationalism, the British were also promising to fulfil Jewish aspirations of a homeland of their own in Western Palestine. In 1917, Arthur Balfour, Foreign Secretary of Lloyd George's administration, made a public announcement in which he stated that, 'His Majesty's government view with favour the establishment in Palestine of a national home for the Jewish people...' The immediate motivation for such a pledge was both to curry favour with leading advisers of American President Woodrow Wilson, who were fervent Zionists, and also to appeal to Jewish financial interests in Britain itself.

The war ended and Britain collected her prize of new imperial possessions in the former Ottoman Empire. The Balfour Declaration proved immensely useful in forestalling Arab demands for independence in Palestine. One of the oldest tricks used by the British to prevent rebellions against their rule in the various countries which they colonised was to turn one set of the inhabitants against another. This worked well in Cyprus, with the Greeks and Turks encouraged to mistrust each other, and also in India with the Muslims and Hindus. In Africa too, the traditional enmity between various tribes could often be exploited to ensure that rather than uniting against the British rulers, they instead dissipated their energies in squabbling between or fighting each other. It is in this context that the British actions in Palestine must be seen.

There is a knack to this kind of thing, which the British had perfected over the years. This entailed keeping hostility between rival groups simmering just below the surface, but preventing it from boiling over into open warfare. In Palestine, the balance was a delicate one and just enough Jews had been allowed to enter the country and settle there, so that the indigenous population would feel threatened and uneasy. Too many though, and the resentments of both sides might become too fierce to suppress and could even erupt into civil war; which was the very situation which arose in the years immediately following the end of the Second World War.

Many survivors of the Holocaust lived for a time after the end of the Second World War in refugee camps, often run by the United Nations. These Displaced Persons camps were scattered across Europe and by and large, those resident there could come and go as they pleased. The Americans, French and Italians were perfectly agreeable to the men, women and children in the camps leaving whenever they felt like it. Ironically enough, it was only the British, who had theoretically established a national home for the Jewish people in Palestine, who put any obstacles in the way of those Jews who wanted to leave the camps and make their way out of Europe.

What the British called 'illegal' immigration to Palestine had been taking place for some years. Ships had been chartered to bring hundred of Jews to the country from as early as 1934. After the end of the war though, the trickle became a flood as Jewish survivors of the camps made their way south through Europe and then chartered, with the aid of sympathetic backers in America and Britain, old ships which would take them from Mediterranean ports to Palestine. The journey was fraught with hazard. One of the first such ships to head for Palestine at the end of the war was the *Mefkure,* which sailed from the Rumanian port of Constanta on 5 August 1945; carrying between 250 and 400 Jews bound for Palestine. For some reason, a Soviet submarine torpedoed the ship and then machine-gunned the survivors. Out of the hundreds of refugees, only five survived.

Despite the danger, other ships began to leave the ports of southern Europe regularly, loaded with as many desperate people as they could carry. At first, the British intercepted the ships when they were able to do so and then interned the passengers in a camp in Palestine. Atlit Camp is shown in Plate 12. Since those treated in this way knew that they had reached their destination and it was probably only a matter of time before they were freed to live in what they saw as their homeland; this strategy did nothing to discourage the 'illegal' immigration.

Other ships carrying varying numbers of Jews arrived off the coast of Palestine over the course of the next year. These ranged from an Italian fishing boat which landed thirty-five people near Caesarea on 28 August 1945 to the *Max Nordau,* which was intercepted by the Royal navy on

13 May 1946 off the coast of Palestine, carrying 1,754 refugees. By the summer of 1946, the British had had enough. They were embroiled in what was beginning to look like a civil war in Palestine between the Jews and Arabs, and the last thing they wanted were large numbers of Jews adding to their problems. On 12 August 1946, a ship called the *Henrietta Szold* was intercepted in the Mediterranean. There were over 500 people on board, all bound for Palestine. Enough was enough, thought the British and that same day made it known that all future 'illegal' immigrants would be detained not in Palestine, but Cyprus. To underline the point, the same day that this announcement was made, the British deported 500 people to Cyprus and locked them into a camp which they had been preparing. They called this action, perhaps ironically, in view of the heat of the Middle eastern summer: Operation Igloo.

The decision to set up concentration camps in Cyprus for survivors of the Holocaust caused a wave of anger among the Jewish community of Palestine. The day after the first refugees were shipped to Cyprus, the Royal Navy stopped two more ships on the high seas. The *Katriel Jaffe*, with 604 passengers, was intercepted by HMS *Talybont*, while at the same time the *Twenty Three*, which had nearly 800 people on board, was taken in charge by HMS *Brissenden*. While these two ships were being boarded, the British were in the process of deporting another 1,300 Jews to Cyprus; loading them onto ships at the port of Haifa. Crowds gathered at the dockside to try and prevent this and soldiers opened fire, killing three people.

The first camp to be opened in Cyprus was at Karaolos, near Famagusta. This had functioned as a prisoner of war camp for Turks during the First World War. Later on, another camp was established at Dekhelia, not far from Larnaca. Nine camps were built altogether; all centred around these two locations. In total, 52,549 people would be detained in these camps between 12 August 1946 and 11 February 1949. Over that time, 1,924 babies were born in the camps.

When the British army first made use of concentration camps, during the Boer War, they blamed the resultant dirt and squalor on the prisoners themselves. The very same tactic was used again in the late 1940s. In October 1946, two months after the first concentration camp was established in Cyprus for Jews, the government in Britain asked for a report on conditions there. They were, understandably, anxious about the impression being made upon the rest of the world by their actions. It is interesting to see what this report said:

> *The immigrants themselves are mostly healthy young adults. The majority have spent a considerable time in enemy concentration camps and are experienced in resistance both passive and active; are very allergic to any form of order or authority and utterly lacking in the most elementary principles of camp sanitation or hygiene.*

There are a number of interesting points here. The first is that this account carefully avoids using the word, 'prisoners', at any point. By talking of 'immigrants', it is possible to maintain the illusion that this is not a prison camp, surrounded by barbed wire and with guards who were quite prepared to open fire on the inmates. On 12 November 1946, for instance, MP Barnett Janner asked the Secretary of State for the Colonies for details of an 'incident' at the camp near Famagusta. He was told that:

> *During the afternoon, the immigrants … made a successful attempt to tear down the perimeter wire and break out of the camp. The situation became extremely dangerous and to restore order the military guard under command of an officer displayed the necessary banner calling upon the people to halt. They did not halt, and certain members of the guard were ordered to fire. Six shots were fired, and two Jews were wounded …*

The second point is that having crammed so many prisoners into such inadequate accommodation, they are then blamed for the resulting, unhygienic conditions.

The final point about the report, quoted above, is the sheer inhumanity of whoever wrote it. Despite knowing full well that most of those being held in the Cyprus camps had already spent a, 'considerable time' in German concentration camps, the author of the report cannot seemingly understand why these same men and women should now be, 'allergic to any form of order or authority'! The irony of the army which defeated the Germans and freed the Jews from their clutches, now in their turn keeping the same people cooped up in concentration camps does not appear to have been noticed by whoever wrote this. These people had, against all the odds, survived the Holocaust, only to find themselves being thrust once more into concentration camps. Little wonder that feelings ran exceedingly high on occasion in the camps.

The similarities between the camps of Cyprus and those in which they had been confined in Nazi Germany, would have been fairly obvious to the inmates and extended even to such things as outbreaks of typhoid; the disease which killed Anne Frank in the concentration camp of Belsen. In July 1947, there were a number of deaths at Karaolos camp from this cause. For those detained there, this must have been a terrible reminder of a past from which they thought that they had escaped.

Some of the actions taken by the British at this time were so thoughtless, that they almost defy belief. It was felt, for example, that it would make it easier to administer the camp at Karaolas if a light railway line could be constructed from the capital of Nicosia; running directly to the camp. Not wishing to pay free workers to build this transport link, the British army struck upon what seemed to them a brilliant piece of cost-cutting. In addition to all the Jews being held prisoner on Cyprus, there were also 5,000 German prisoners of war. Why not use these men as labourers? Could it really be that the British administrators who came up with this scheme knew nothing about the railway lines running to death camps such as Auschwitz and Treblinka? Did they honestly not see what a truly shocking sight it would be to the survivors of the Holocaust being held captive in the camps of Cyprus to see squads of German soldiers building a railway line to their camp? At the very least, such an action argues for an appalling degree of insensitivity on the part of the officials who gave the go-ahead for this project.

The prisoners held on Cyprus were officially classified by the British as prisoners of war. This was a strange way of looking at things, since all these men, women and children had arrived peacefully and unarmed in the Middle East, seeking only refuge from the horrors of war. The idea that they were in some sense enemy combatants seems today almost beyond belief. Never the less, it was on this basis that they were placed in camps and held under armed guard. In defence of the British, it may be said that although conditions in the camps were primitive and harsh, the detainees were largely left to their own devices; with the British guards making no attempt to interfere in the actual running of the camps. They supplied accommodation, food and water; but left the administration of the camps to the Jews themselves. The only real restriction upon them was that they were hemmed in by barbed wire and that if any attempt was made to break out, then it was liable to be met with the use of lethal force. This happened on 18 April 1947.

As part of what they conceived their duty to be, towards the Mandate Territory of Palestine, the British were determined to limit to 750 the number of Jews whom they allowed into the country each month. It was seen as a good idea if the monthly quota of 750 was drawn from those detained in the camps on Cyprus; being composed chiefly of women and children. There was good reason for this, in that the British were determined not to allow any young men of military age into Palestine, lest they immediately take up arms against either the British army of occupation or the Arabs, with whom many Jewish settlers were engaged in what would soon flare up into open war.

By 18 April 1947, the quota of 750 Jews who were due to be transported 'legally' to Palestine from the camp at Karaolos, had been waiting long enough. They were overdue to leave the camp and it was thought that the British were deliberately delaying matters. When the time finally came for the fortunate 750 to leave the camp, it was announced suddenly that fewer than half that number would be leaving, due to transport problems. At this point, a riot erupted. Buildings throughout the camp were set on fire and a concerted effort was made to break down the barbed wire fence surrounding the camp. It looked to the army as though a mass breakout was in progress and the order was given to open fire. One prisoner was killed and another half dozen wounded, before the rush at the fence was beaten back. Later that day, tanks were brought to the vicinity of Karaolos and it was made clear to those in the camp that there would be no hesitation in using armoured vehicles against them, should the need arise. A few days later, more troops were sent to the area and some of the prisoners began a hunger strike.

Three months after the death of the prisoner during the attempt to break out of the Karaolas camp came one of the most notorious incidents in the struggle between the British government and the Holocaust survivors. This entailed the British army setting up two new concentration camps for Jews in Germany itself.

In 1928, a passenger ship called the SS *President Warfield* was launched in America by the Baltimore Steam Packet Company. For the next fourteen years, the SS *Warfield* transported passengers and freight between the ports of Virginia, Baltimore and Maryland. When the Second World War began, the ship was pressed into military service, before later being disposed of to the Potomac Shipwrecking Company in 1946. From there, it was transferred to a Jewish organisation which was arranging for the transport from Europe to Palestine of those Jews hoping to enter their historic homeland.

In the early hours of 11 July 1947, the SS *Warfield,* renamed the *Exodus 1947,* left the south of France; containing over 4,500 Jewish refugees. Among them were 1,283 women and 1,672 children. Ostensibly, the destination was the Turkish port of Istanbul but nobody had any illusions at all about where the *Exodus* was really headed; especially not the British, who immediately began shadowing the *Exodus* with the warship HMS *Mermaid.* By the time that the *Exodus* was twenty miles or so from the coast of Palestine, the British had made the decision to intercept the ship. This was little short of piracy, as the *Exodus* was still in international waters. In the fighting which ensued during the boarding, three Jews were shot dead.

Having seized control of the *Exodus,* it was decided to take it to the port of Haifa, which was then in British-occupied Palestine. Once there, all the passengers and crew were transferred to three other ships, which the following day set sail for France. The British had decided that since these people had set out from France, then that was where they would be returned to. When the three ships containing the passengers from the *Exodus* arrived off the coast of France near Marseilles a fortnight later, the intention was to demonstrate to the others tempted to try and enter

Palestine 'illegally', just how pointless the whole exercise could be. Here were 4,500 people who had taken ship three weeks ago and were now back where they had started.

The only problem for the British was that the men, women and children refused to disembark and the French made it plain that they would not countenance the use of force to dump people in their country. An *impasse* had been reached. After three weeks of deliberations, the British government made the inhuman decision that if these people would not do as they were told, then they would be taken back to the scene of their awful suffering and locked up once again in concentration camps. The ships now set off again; this time heading for Hamburg in northern Germany. Diplomats in the British Embassy in Paris warned the Foreign Office in London that this was turning into a public relations disaster, but 'Operation Oasis', as the plan to send the Jews back to Germany was called, was launched anyway. A diplomat at the British embassy cabled London, warning that, 'Our opponents in France and, I dare say in other countries, have made great play with the fact that these immigrants were being kept behind barbed wire, in concentration camps and guarded by Germans'.

As Operation Oasis unfolded, Britain was widely criticised for their treatment of these ordinary people who had suffered so much as a result of the actions of Hitler's Germany. When they arrived at Hamburg, the men on board the three ships simply refused to leave and so hundreds of British soldiers were sent to subdue them. During the fighting, a number of injuries were caused to those being removed from the boats. Having got them ashore, the 4,500 refugees, most of whom had already been in German concentration camps, now experienced the novelty of being locked instead inside British concentration camps. There were two camps, both near Lubeck; Am Stau and Poppendorf.

Foreign correspondents described the camps to which the passengers from the *Exodus* were sent as being indistinguishable from concentration camps and they were probably right. One of the camps had been designed to hold 1,000 people and now 2,500 were crammed into it, mostly living in tents. The prisoners were not badly treated, but there was no mistaking the fact that they were being held against their will. The daily calorific intake was just 2,800 per person; which was just about sufficient to maintain health. So strong was the condemnation in the overseas press, particular the American newspapers, that the government in London contacted the army commanders in the field, to seek assurances that it was not true that Germans were being used to guard the prisoners in the camps at Lubeck.

If the aim of shipping 4,000 Holocaust survivors back to Europe in this way and locking them up in camps in Germany was to discourage others from making the journey to Palestine, then those who carried out this cruel act were to learn that they had dramatically misjudged the mood of the displaced Jews. By the time that the State of Israel was founded, in May 1948, sixty-five ships arrived in the Eastern Mediterranean from Europe. These contained a total of 69,878 'illegal' immigrants; all of whom had as their intention settling in their historic homeland.

As the months passed, with no sign of any decline in the numbers attempting to reach Palestine, so too did the situation in that country slip into chaos and disorder. It was becoming abundantly plain to the British that there was little chance of their being able to maintain a grip on Palestine and so the decision was made by the government in London to divest themselves of their responsibilities as neatly as could be done, given the circumstances. Even now, when they were about to leave, the British were still working out how they might be able to continue having some influence in that part of the Eastern Mediterranean. Twenty years earlier, some 80 per cent of Palestine had been detached from the area covered by the League of nations Mandate and given to an Arab chieftain to whom the British owed a favour. This was the kingdom of Transjordan; later to be called simply 'Jordan'. The army of Transjordan was commanded by a British officer and it was felt that even after a withdrawal from Palestine, it might be possible to maintain a hold onto parts of the country via this proxy.

Britain requested the newly formed United Nations, the body which had taken over from the League of Nations, to come up with a proposal for Palestine, so that the British could relinquish the mandate granted to them by the League. This 'Committee of Study' met from May to September in 1947. It recommended the partition of Palestine into independent Jewish and Arab states. This led to the establishment of a second United Nations group called the United Nations Special Committee on Palestine; more commonly known as UNSCOP for short. The British were still trying to keep the lid on the conflict in Palestine, but at the first meeting of UNSCOP, which took place near New York on 25 September 1947, the British Colonial Secretary made his country's position plain. Arthur Creech Jones told the committee that Britain was no longer prepared to have any sort of involvement in Palestine. British forces would, in the event of an escalation of violence withdraw their forces at the first opportunity.

If the British game had been a straight one, then those in the camps of Cyprus might have thought at this point that their days of captivity were almost over. If the British armed forces were going to be withdrawn and the British administration dissolved, then surely there could be no further reason to hold them? This would have made perfect sense if the British were being completely open about their intentions. In the event though, despite the British assurance in the autumn of 1947 that they were pulling out, it was to be 1949 before all the prisoners in Cyprus were to be freed from the camps.

On 29 November 1947, the General Assembly of the United Nations adopted a plan which would set up a Jewish and Arab state in Palestine. Over the next few months, a civil war developed and the British army prepared to leave the country. The League of Nations mandate under which Britain ruled the country expired on 14 May 1948. On that same day, the State of Israel was declared and within minutes, the United States had recognised the provisional government set up there. The first country in the world to grant *de jure* recognition of Israel in 17 May 1948 was the Union of Soviet Socialist Republics.

The setting up of the Jewish state did not put an end to the civil war which had been raging. Quite the opposite, in fact, because various Arab countries such as Syria, Egypt and Transjordan now invaded Palestine, seeking new territory of their own which could be annexed. Transjordan managed to seize the lion's share of the new nation, by occupying the areas of Judea and Samaria. Instead of helping the Palestinian Arabs to found their own country, the Emir of Transjordan promptly announced

the annexation of the land which he and his British allies had managed
to snatch.

While the fledgling nation of Israel was fighting for its very survival,
the British government was still determined to avoid doing anything
which might aid those they regarded as enemies. They had for years
been locking up any Jews trying to reach Israel and now, even though
they were withdrawing from Palestine themselves, they still did their best
to prevent the Jews from setting up their own country, as the United
Nations had agreed they should. Just when every single man was vital
to the New army of Israel, Britain chose to keep all Jews of military age
whom they held on Cyprus, in the concentration camps. Thousands of
men whose presence could have meant the difference between victory
and defeat in the War of Independence, were kept under lock and key for
the entire duration of the war. It was not until February the following
year that the camps were emptied and all the prisoners allowed to leave
Cyprus for Israel.

In the meantime, a month after the State of Israel declared its
independence, the British were still holding 24,000 able-bodied Jewish
men in the camps of Cyprus, so that they did not join in the war raging
throughout the former territory of British occupied Palestine. This was
on the grounds that the British government wished to be seen as strictly
neutral; not taking any action which might be seen to favour one side
or another in the conflict. The hypocrisy of this supposed position was
truly breathtaking. The Arab Legion, the army of Transjordan, was busily
engaged in grabbing as much land as possible from the former mandated
territory. The commander of the Arab legion since 1939 had of course
been Lieutenant-General Sir John Bagot Glubb; a senior officer in the
British army. Nothing could more clearly demonstrate the partiality of
the British during the savage war which followed the departure of their
forces, nor the double standards which caused them to continue holding
tens of thousands of Jews in concentration camps; men who now had a
country of their own to which they wished to go.

The dreadful behaviour of the British government was the object of
remark not only in the American newspapers and other foreign press,
but was also raised in the House of Commons. To defend their position,

the British took to portraying the Jewish prisoners as communists and terrorists. Increasingly desperate to leave the camps and join the new country which was in danger of being over-run and destroyed almost as soon as it had come into being, a number of mass escapes were attempted from camps such as Karaolas. On 9 October 1948, five months after the creation of Israel, fifteen prisoners tried to break out of Karaolas. Their intentions could hardly have been plainer. They wished only to leave Cyprus and travel to help Israel in her struggle for survival. The British administration of Cyprus though, could see what these men were really up to!

There had been clashes in Cyprus in the late 1940s, not only between Greeks and Turks, but also left and right wing activists. The British in Cyprus thought, or purported to believe, that the escape attempts from the camps were part of this ideological struggle; rather than the simple determination of prisoners to travel to join their fellow-Jews in Israel. The suggestion was made officially that the men in the camps were dominated by communists and that if fighting broke out in Cyprus between different political factions, then a mass escape from the concentration camps would see thousands of Jews joining the fight on the side of the left-wingers. It was a mad fantasy; another excuse to avoid releasing the prisoners.

When prisoners *were* freed from the camps, they were subjected to such indignities as having their luggage hacked to pieces by British soldiers on the almost unbelievable grounds that they might be hiding escapees in their suitcases! This scenario was seriously advanced in parliament on 10 November 1948 by Colonial Secretary Arthur Creech Jones. On that day Mr Janner, the Member of Parliament for Leicester West, rose in the Commons and asked why those being permitted to leave the camps in Cyprus were having their luggage broken open by soldiers with bayonets and the contents scattered. The Secretary of State for the Colonies had two good explanations for this conduct by the British forces in Cyprus. In the first place, the luggage might contain 'stolen property'. What on earth those leaving the camps might be trying to steal, he did not say.

There was, according to Mr Creech Jones, the possibility that one of the women or children being freed because they were not of military age, could try and smuggle out an able-bodied young man in their luggage.

This suggestion was, unsurprisingly, greeted with incredulity by many MPs. Mr J. Lewis, the Labour member for Bolton, asked a very pertinent question. He said, 'When it is suspected that a person of military age is concealed in a package, is it the practice to pierce the package with a bayonet?' There was no reply to this question.

It was not until February 1949 that the last Jewish prisoners being held by the British in the camps of Cyprus were freed. By that time, the war in Palestine was over and the Arab Legion of Transjordan had, with British help, been able to annex the area known today as the 'West Bank'. Only Britain and Pakistan ever recognised this flagrant violation of the United Nations plan for the country.

The opening by Britain of concentration camps for Jews was a shameful coda to the Holocaust. Almost all of those held in these camps had previously been prisoners in Nazi camps and although it might have seemed a neat solution to the pressing problem of the 'illegal' immigration to Palestine, the camps were both a public relations disaster for Britain and also an act of terrible cruelty to men and women who had already suffered unspeakable horrors during the Second World War. The lesson learned by Britain from their use of such camps, so soon after the revelations of Belsen and Dachau, was not perhaps the most ethical that could have been hoped for. Rather than decide that concentration camps were a wicked tool to use, the British came to the conclusion that the large-scale use of camps would be perfectly acceptable, provided always that nobody actually referred to them as 'concentration camps'. When next they needed to make use of such camps, less than five years after the closure of Karaolas and the eight other camps in Cyprus, the decision was taken sedulously to avoid talking of camps at all. This, it was hoped, would prevent criticism.

Chapter 8

1948-1960
Calling a Spade a Manual Digging
Implement: The Malayan Emergency

Extreme sensitivity about use of the term 'concentration camp' after the end of the Second World War led on occasion to ludicrous circumlocution, particularly from the British. After the images of Belsen and Auschwitz had seared themselves into the public consciousness in the late 1940s, nobody, least of all the British government, wished to be accused of running concentration camps. This resulted in bizarre situations developing in the post-war years, as the British army ran hundreds of concentration camps, without once using the dreaded expression itself. The camps full of Jews in Cyprus were of course concentration camps in all but name, but less than a decade later, an even stranger example of this studied avoidance of calling things by their right name occurred in South-East Asia.

In 1900 and 1901, the British army rounded up all those living in various parts of South Africa and took them to live in large camps, where the prisoners would be unable to offer support or assistance to the guerrilla fighters opposing the British. These places were called, quite correctly, concentration camps, and about 250,000 people were held in them. In the 1950s, the British army conducted a precisely similar operation, when they took a quarter of Malaya's Chinese population from their homes and kept them behind barbed wire, so that they too would be unable to offer comfort or aid to guerrillas. This operation involved over twice as many people as were detained during the Boer War; some half a million Chinese villagers being placed behind barbed wire fences, with armed guards patrolling the perimeters of the camps. This time though, instead of calling the sites 'concentration camps', the British designated them as

'New Villages'. It was a brilliant propaganda coup; simply by avoiding talk of 'concentration camps', the British were able to set up and run a network consisting of 450 concentration camps and nobody batted an eyelid. Terminology was everything and as long as everybody called the compounds 'New Villages', it appeared that nobody, other than the Chinese themselves, would raise any objections.

Not only that, but the brutal campaign of suppression mounted by the British army against the Chinese guerrillas in Malaya is remembered today as an example of a humane operation; best summed up by the phrase coined by the governor of the country; a ruthless military man. We remember Malaya today for the expression, 'Hearts and Minds'.

When the Japanese invaded neighbouring countries such as Indochina and Malaya, the only ones who fought tenaciously against the occupations were not the colonial British and French forces who had been running these countries, but the indigenous inhabitants themselves. After the Japanese had been defeated during the Second World War, those who had been fighting guerrilla wars believed, not unreasonably, that the old, colonial order was ended. Having rid themselves of Japanese overlords, they did not feel in the least inclined to see them replaced by French or British masters.

The European powers were slow to react to what British Prime Minister Harold Macmillan later referred to, in another context, as 'the wind of change' and from the late 1940s onwards tried to reassert their hegemony in the Far East. For the French, this was to prove disastrous, as they struggled against the communist led insurgency in Indochina; the country now known as Vietnam. The war against the guerrilla army of Ho Chi Minh culminated in 1954 with the siege of Dien Bien Phu, which was a humiliating defeat for the French army. Shortly afterwards, the French abandoned all title to Indochina and withdrew their armed forces.

The British experience in Malaya played out very differently. Just as in French Indochina, the guerrillas fighting the Japanese occupiers were predominantly communists. The Malayan People's Anti-Japanese Army (MPAJA) was led by the Malayan Communist Party. The actual achievements of the MPAJA, in terms of casualties and damage caused to the occupying Japanese forces are questionable, but there can be no doubt that they maintained an insurgency from 1942 until the end of the war in 1945.

Among those in the MPAJA, and also a member of the communist party, was a teenager called Chin Peng, who acted as a liaison officer with the British army. From time to time, submarines would land troops on the coast of Malaya and Chin Peng would meet them and lead them to the MPAJA bases. For this work, at the end of the war Chin Peng was decorated by the British, being awarded two campaign medals; the Burma Star and the 1939-1945 War medal. He was also appointed OBE. Considering that he was only twenty years of age at the end of the Second World War, this indicates that Chin Peng was probably a remarkable young man. In 1945, he was invited to London and took part in the victory march.

Like most members of both the MPAJA and the Malayan Communist Party, Chin Peng was ethnically Chinese. For historical reasons, there were so many Chinese and Indians living in Malaya during the 1940s, that the Malayans themselves made up only half the population of their own country. Approximately 40 per cent of the people in Malaya were of Chinese origin. The Japanese seemed to have a visceral distrust of Chinese people and the Chinese suffered more hardship during the Japanese occupation of Malaya than did ethnic Malayans. This might account, at least in part, or the fact that the MPAJA was dominated by the Chinese.

For a couple of months after the end of the Second World War in the summer of 1945, the MPAJA exercised *de facto* control over the country. This meant that Malaya effectively had a communist government, something which neither the British nor the Americans relished. In the autumn, the British returned, thanked the MPAJA again for all their help and then once more took up the reins of colonial governance. It is hardly to be wondered at that many of the former guerrilla fighters felt, to say the least of it, a little irritated by this attitude.

One might ask why the British were so keen to regain control in Malaya. It must have been obvious to most people that the days of the British Empire were over and indeed the British were retreating from many of the countries which had at one time been seen as vital to their interests. Even India was being abandoned. Malaya though was a very profitable country to occupy, particularly for its tin mines and rubber plantations. There seemed no point in walking away from such a valuable possession. Like the French in Indochina, the British decided to stay on and override any protest by use of their military prowess. Surely well-trained European armies would be more than adequate to suppress any uprising by a band of ragged terrorists? The difficulty was, of course, that greater forces were now at work in this part of the world than had been the case before the beginning of the Second World War. South-East Asia was becoming the front line in the geopolitical struggle for dominance which was to become known as the Cold War. In China, the communist forces of Mao Tse Tung were about to triumph and the Soviet Union was also flexing its muscles in Europe and the Far East. This meant that the underground armies, led by communists, in Indochina and Malaya, were in a sense acting as the proxies of the mighty Soviet empire. The balance between the Commonwealth armies fighting the Malayan insurgency and the guerrillas against whom their operations were directed was not nearly as one-sided as it might appear on the surface.

Apart from the support of the Soviet Union and later China, the domestic situation in Malaya itself lent support to the communist cause. The economic benefits of exporting rubber and tin went to the planters and mine owners, who were in the main British. The ordinary workers were Chinese and Malay and it was upon their labour that the profits of the British companies were built. On 29 January 1946, the Malayan Communist Party organised a 24-hour general strike, which served to alert the British to the danger which they faced from their former allies. The following year, more than 300 strikes were organised by the communists in Malaya.

While this industrial and political activity was being undertaken, the communists were organising themselves into a military organisation, aiming to drive the British from the country and conduct the same sort of guerrilla warfare against them as the MPAJA had against the Japanese only a few years earlier. The new groups, which was essentially a second incarnation of the MPAJA, was known by several names, including the

Malayan National Liberation Army, Malayan People's Liberation Army and the Malayan Races Liberation Army. For the sake of clarity, the Malayan Races Liberation Army or MRLA will be used throughout.

The opening shots in what was to become, for all intents and purposes, a civil war, were fired on 16 June 1948. In what became known as the Sungai Siput Incident, three European managers of rubber plantations were shot dead. Mr A.E. Walker, manager of the Elphil Estate was killed at his desk at 8.30am. Half an hour later, John Alison, manager of the Phin Soon Estate was also shot dead, as was his assistant, Ian Christian. Two days after the murders, on 18 June 1948, a State of Emergency was declared by the administration in Malaya.

It might at first seem that describing the onset of a guerrilla war as an 'emergency' is an example of the British fondness for euphemism; a bit like calling the thirty-year-long civil war in Northern Ireland, 'The Troubles'. In the case of the Malaya Emergency though, there were sound financial reasons for ensuring that the word 'war' was never used in connection with the fighting which developed over the succeeding years. The plantations and tin mines were all insured by British companies. Most policies have clauses which exclude payment for damage caused by war. It was therefore in nobody's interests to have the situation in Malaya called a war at any time; even when the Australian air force was dropping 500-pound bombs on the rebels.

Plate 14 shows an Australian bomber in action in Malaya in 1950. In many ways, the Malayan Emergency can be seen as a practice run or rehearsal for the later American war in Vietnam; although with less catastrophic consequences for those embroiled in it. The heavy bombers, relentless pursuit of communist guerrillas hiding in the jungles of South-East Asia, even the use of defoliants such as Agent Orange; all these tactics were part of the war being waged against the communist insurgents of Malaya in the late 1940s and early 1950s. The photograph of the bomber is of particular interest. In addition to their complete failure to mention concentration camps in connection with the Malayan Emergency, modern writers often talk of the success of a strategy of, 'Winning Hearts and Minds'. It is little short of grotesque to see such a distortion of history. Holding half a million civilians in concentration camps, launching bombing raids and the destroying crops with defoliants were what won the war for the British. Whether these methods actually won any hearts and minds is open to question; it was military force which won the day.

The problems faced by the British army and the solutions which they adopted both bore uncanny similarities to the events of the Boer War, half a century earlier. The same tactics had worked then and there was no reason to suppose that they would not work again. However, a lot had changed since the war in South Africa. Then, most people in Britain had been unsympathetic to the Boers and indifferent to the fact that many were being detained in concentration camps. With the newsreel films of the liberation of Belsen still fresh in the minds of the British population though, it would have been impolitic to talk of concentrating the population of Malaya in camps. Hence the wonderful euphemism of the New Villages and the slogan of 'Winning Hearts and Minds'.

Very soon after the beginning of the insurgency, it became fairly clear that the guerrillas, or terrorists as the British called them, were relying heavily upon the aid and support of their countrymen. Many of the Chinese in Malaya lived on the edge of the jungle, in settlements on land to which they had no legal title. These villagers were known as 'squatters' and there were hundreds of thousands of them. Just as in the Boer War, this civilian population supplied the guerrillas with both information and food. In South Africa, the Boer guerrillas moved about the vast open spaces and were very hard to track down. The MRLA had their bases in the jungle and it was all but impossible for them to be found by British army patrols. They would emerge, carry out sabotage on mines and communications and then slip back into the jungle. The Chinese 'squatters' were organised by the communists directing the MRLA into a support network called 'Min Yuan'. They would thus be supplied with food and intelligence by a willing network of supporters.

The challenges faced by the British army in tackling the Malayan insurgency were so similar to those faced during the Boer War that it was perhaps inevitable that the same solutions should be applied. Having tried, without any great success, to flush the guerrilla fighters out of the jungle, the plan was formulated to remove their support network and so starve them into submission. This would of course entail preventing the guerrillas from receiving any support from their fellow countrymen who were farming the land alongside the jungle.

In October 1948, four months after the beginning of the so-called Emergency, a veteran, colonial administrator was appointed High Commissioner for Malaya. Sir Henry Lovell Goldsworthy Gurney took up his post on 1 October 1948. For the next two years, the insurgency gathered pace and nobody seemed to have the wit or determination to tackle it effectively. In 1950, a new Director of Operations arrived in Malaya. Lieutenant-general Harold Rawdon Briggs was a career soldier who had been called from retirement in Cyprus to devise a plan which would settle the problems in Malaya once and for all.

It did not take Lieutenant-General Briggs long to come up with a plan, which became known, unsurprisingly as 'The Briggs' Plan'. The problem, as Briggs saw it, was that the guerrillas were being fed and provided with a good deal of intelligence by the half million or so Chinese villagers who were scattered along the edges of the jungle. Remove those people and the MRLA would find themselves with food and lacking the information so vital to planning ambushes and evading the operations of the army searching for them. The solution that Briggs came up with was to concentrate all these people where they could be kept under guard and prevented from sharing food with members of the MRLA or indeed even being allowed to talk to them.

It can hardly be wondered at that the government in London was a little cautious at first of adopting the Briggs' Plan. The idea of 'concentrating' populations in convenient locations was just that little bit closer to 'concentration camps' than was politically comfortable. The last thing that the Labour government then in power wished to be seen doing was setting up concentration camps! However, it was clearly the best strategy for ending the conflict and so in 1950, the administration in Malaya began implementing it.

Before the building of the New Villages, a number of other methods had been adopted to discourage support for the MRLA. Some of them seem quite shocking today, especially when we recall the famous legend about winning the 'hearts and minds' of the population. In May 1950, the British War Minister, John Strachey, visited Malaya and while he was there, new measures were announced to tackle the guerrillas. For example, the death penalty was introduced from 2 June 1950 for anybody collecting subscriptions for the communist party. Those involved in making supplies available for the guerrillas also faced execution. Being found in possession of arms had been a capital offence since the Emergency had been declared two years earlier and a number of men had already been hanged for this. In May 1949, an Indian Trade Union organiser called Mr Ganapathy was executed for being found with a revolver and six rounds of ammunition. On 23 June 1950, five Chinese guerrillas were hanged together, after a gun battle with the police. Even relatively trifling things could result in ferocious punishment under the emergency regulations. In December 1952, a 22-year-old worker on a rubber plantation called Sia Kim Chee, was sentenced to ten years hard labour in the High Court at Kuala Lumpar. His crime? Being found in possession of a pair of wire cutters, which it was thought he might have been planning to give to the guerrillas.

Executions and heavy prison sentences were not sufficient in themselves to halt the uprising and so in early 1951, the rounding up and deportation of the Chinese squatters to the 'New Villages' began. Already, thousands of captured suspects were being detained without trial in prison camps. By the spring of 1951, when the Briggs' Plan was under way, 11,000 suspected terrorists were being held in camps. At the end of March, 120,000 squatters had been uprooted from their homes and sent to New Villages. Another 3-400,000 were to follow.

This whole operation, undertaken during what was effectively a war and affecting hundreds of thousands of civilians, was absolutely forbidden by the Fourth Geneva Convention. The real reason for the forced removal of so many people from their homes was that the army suspected that some villagers were helping the rebels by supplying them with both practical help in the form of food and also providing them with intelligence on troop movements and so on. This meant that the moving of entire villages to new, fortified compounds was a form of collective punishment. Articles 33 and 49 of the Geneva Convention make it quite clear that both collective punishments and the deportation of civilian populations in this way are war crimes.

The High Commissioner of Malaya, Sir Henry Gurney, liked to relax and play a few rounds of golf when the pressures of his office allowed him time. For this purpose, he used to visit a hill resort called Fraser's Hill; 3,000 feet above sea level, with fresh, cool air and various amenities such as a country club and golf course. On 6 October 1951, Sir Henry was travelling along the road to Fraser's Hill, accompanied by his wife and his private secretary; a man called Staples. Security was tight. In addition to the Rolls-Royce in which Sir Henry was travelling with his wife and secretary, an armoured scout car rode ahead of the High Commissioner's car and behind it were both a police wireless van, which remained in touch with the army, and a Land Rover containing six Malay police officers.

As the convoy made its way into the hills north of Kuala Lumpur, the wireless van developed mechanical trouble and broke down. Sir Henry was advised to call off the trip to Fraser's Hill, but insisted that he wished to press on regardless. The convoy travelled a further eight miles and then, rounding a bend in the road, found themselves under attack from thirty-eight members of the MRLA, who were laying in wait for them. The High Commissioner's car was raked with machine gun fire, which killed the chauffeur and five of the six police officers travelling in the Land Rover were also wounded. The guerrillas were equipped with both .303 Bren guns and also Sten sub-machine guns. In an act of incredible bravery, Sir Henry pushed his wife and private secretary to the floor of the car and then jumped out, running towards the attackers in an effort to draw their fire. He was successful in this, as all the gunmen began firing at him immediately.

When the shooting began, the driver of the armoured scout car decided that the best course of action would be to race on ahead and fetch reinforcements. He drove at high speed to the nearest police post and then returned with a body of police. When they reached the scene of the ambush, it was to find the High Commissioner dead. His gallant action had saved the lives of his wife and secretary. According to Chin Peng, the communist leader, the ambush on the road to Fraser's Hill was a routine one and it was only by the sheerest chance that the guerrillas found themselves assassinating the High Commissioner.

By the time of the High Commissioner's assassination, implementation of the Briggs' Plan was in full swing. Essentially, it was exactly the same strategy that General Weyles had used in Cuba in the 1890s and also identical to the British treatment of Boer civilians during the South African war half-a-century earlier. The ordinary population was to be isolated from the guerrillas and all contact prevented. There were two main reasons for the creation of the New Villages and the moving of almost the entire Chinese 'squatter' population into them.

The Chinese peasants known as the squatters were spread out along the edge of the jungle. It was impossible to say which of them might be guerrillas and which simply small-scale farmers, tending their fields and minding their own business. The communist guerrillas moved in and out of the Chinese settlements, collecting food, information and recruits as and when they needed them. It was a nightmare for the British forces, because it meant that the guerrillas were so embedded in the civilian population that they could never correctly be identified.

The first thing that uprooting these farmers and 'concentrating' them in fortified enclosures achieved, was to prevent eager young men from drifting off to join the MRLA whenever the mood took them. Entry to and exit from to the camps, the so-called 'New Villages', was strictly controlled by the police and army. The second way in which these camps hampered the guerrillas was by forbidding them access to the food which they needed and with which the Chinese farmers had been supplying them. They were also unable to use the squatters as their eyes and ears; learning about the movements and disposition of military forces.

The procedure for implementing the Briggs' Plan was simple and brutal. A 'squatter' village would be surrounded by heavily armed troops and the inhabitants given a short time to collect their belongings. They would then be loaded onto lorries. As they drove off, they might see their old homes being burned down, to prevent anybody else trying to live there. They were taken to stockades surrounded by barbed wire and with searchlights which swept the area outside the compound at night, so as to see if anybody was escaping or attacking. The paddy fields associated with each New Village lay outside the perimeter fence and when the Chinese were allowed out for the day to cultivate their fields, they were searched by soldiers or police officers. This was to see if they might be carrying any food, messages, weapons or anything else that might be of use to the guerrillas of the MRLA.

As far as imprisonment went, this was not an especially onerous existence, but it was plain that those living in the New Villages were viewed by the British as *being* prisoners; people who were under constant observation and supervision. It was a very different life from that which these people had enjoyed in their own settlements.

The New Villages themselves were clean and well constructed; consisting of rows of neat huts, with concrete paths and plots of land to cultivate outside the fence. Materially, they were certainly no worse than the villages where the Chinese squatters had previously been living. Indeed, in some ways, they could be considered an improvement. Electricity and piped water were laid on, which most of the older homes on the edge of the jungle lacked. As a matter of fact, 1.2 million people today still live in the New Villages which were built as part of the Brigg's Plan.

The new buildings to which the Chinese had been forcibly resettled might have had all mod-cons, but there was one crucial difference between the New Villages and the settlements where they had previously been living. This was the stout wire netting fences, topped with barbed wire, which encircled every one of the New Villages. The gates to these enclosures were locked at night and watchtowers and armed guards ensured that nobody entered or left unless the authorities were aware of it. Even the suspicion that somebody was intending to breach the security of these sites brought the most savage punishment from the colonial authorities. Sia Kim Chee, the man who was sent to prison for ten years in 1952 for possessing a pair of wire cutters, was treated so harshly because it was thought that he might have been helping communists enter villages by cutting the fence.

It is fascinating to compare the official version of what was being done to the Chinese peasants in Malaya with the realities of the process. Very early on, the British government realised that here was something which could backfire upon them in the most spectacular way. Confining half a million people in concentration camps, only six years after the end the

Second World War, could certainly generate some negative publicity. So it was that in September 1950, Hugh Carleton Greene, brother of the novelist Graham Greene, arrived in Malaya to take charge of the newly formed Emergency Information Services. This body was set up to produce and disseminate propaganda on behalf of the British administration and armed forces in the country. The first film made by Greene must rank as an absolute classic of its kind and it is all but impossible to watch it today without bursting into laughter. It is beyond parody.

A New Life – Squatter Resettlement is like a pastiche of the public information films so popular in the 1950s. The voiceover is breezy and spoken in clipped and authoritative English. Cheerful background music ebbs and swells as we see the wonderful new life of the men and women who have, for their own good, been evicted from their homes. As the narrator explains:

> *The squatter has long had a hard struggle to raise food for himself and his family. But when the bandits took refuge in the jungle, they were able to steal his food; for the police could not protect him where he lived. The emergency powers had two squatter problems to solve. How to defend these defenceless people and how to ensure that their food is not feeding the terrorists.*

The film shows kindly British officials planning how best to improve the harsh lives of the squatters, coming up with the idea of 'protecting' them from terrorism by destroying their homes and forcing them into concentration camps. After shots of a 'New Village' being prepared, the camera team go to a squatter village and watch the forced removal of the inhabitants to a guarded compound:

> *The time has come for the squatters to be told that they must leave their homes. With all the promises of new homes for old and a new life for the old, terrorist-haunted insecurity, it is still hard for some of them to make the break. This has been their home for so long. They do not at first understand why they must leave. Packing up too is a sad business.*

The above voiceover was accompanied by heartbreaking scenes of miserable-looking Chinese families being chivvied about by soldiers and forced to board lorries, to be transported to their new homes.

According to Hugh Carleton Greene's masterly production, the whole resettlement programme had been undertaken in a spirit of compassion for the plight of the squatters themselves. Reports from the army gave a somewhat different view of life for the Chinese villagers, however. In April 1952, for example, collective punishment was imposed on the village of Sengei Pelek. Far from being terrorised by 'bandits' and having their food stolen, those living at Sengei Pelek had gone to great lengths to share their rations with the guerrillas. They managed this despite being searched by soldiers every time they left the village. The measures taken against the 4,000 villagers, for supplying food to the insurgents and refusing to inform the authorities of their whereabouts, were severe. A new chain-link fence was erected around the entire village, in an effort to prevent any contact between those living there and the guerrillas of the MRLA. A curfew was also instituted and, worst of all, a 40 per cent reduction in the rice ration was imposed. This was a serious matter to a population living on the edge of starvation as it was. When a similar punitive exercise was carried out at the town of Tanjong Malim, a month earlier, the London School of Hygiene and Tropical Medicine was so concerned that they contacted the Colonial Office, warning that, 'This measure is bound to result in an increase, not only of sickness, but also of deaths, particularly amongst the mothers and very young children'.

For many of those forced to move to the New Villages, life was, materially at least, an improvement on what they had been used to. However comfortable the conditions and regardless of the convenience involved, imprisonment is still imprisonment, though. The wholesale deportation of a civilian population in this way and their confinement in guarded compounds is, quite rightly, viewed today as a crime against humanity. When Germany and the Soviet Union engaged in such practices, many in the West were appalled. The resettlement of the Chinese peasantry in Malay during the early 1950s was precisely the same kind of crime.

Quite apart from the forced resettlement, another part of the implementation of the Briggs' Plan was without any doubt at all a war crime. This was the wholesale destruction of the homes of those who were being moved into the New Villages. To make sure that none of the fighters of the MRLA could make any use of the abandoned villages from which the inhabitants had been driven, the army burned the houses and dug up any crops. Destruction of property in this way is forbidden by the Geneva Convention, which states clearly that destroying homes in this way is only permissible when strictly necessary from a military viewpoint during war.

In fact both the deportation of the squatters to other areas and the destruction of their homes are specifically forbidden by the Fourth Geneva Convention, which came into force on 12 August 1949. Britain signed this convention and had promised to abide by its conditions. They certainly knew that their actions were direct violations of the Geneva Convention. Articles 33 and 34 of the Convention, for instance, forbid the indiscriminate destruction of property and the taking of hostages. Article 49 went on to forbid the deportation of the civilian population. The only way that the British could carry out their operations in Malaya was to maintain the fiction that they were not really fighting a war at all. Of course, most people would say that when your air force is dropping thousands of tonnes of bombs on an enemy, then a *de facto* state of war exists and that it would be absurd to think otherwise. Thinking of a comparable campaign, would it be reasonable to deny that the Americans fought a war in Vietnam, simply because there was no formal declaration to this effect? It seems though that the British government might genuinely have persuaded themselves that what they were up to in Malaya during the 1950s did not really amount to a war.

That the fighting in Malaya was not regarded as being a war may be seen when we consider some of the atrocities committed by the British troops. Having killed guerrillas in the course of jungle fighting, the soldiers did not wish to drag their bodies all the way back to base so that they could be identified; their features being checked against various photographs in wanted posters. The solution seemed obvious and it became common practice simply to hack off the heads of the dead Chinese fighters and then carry them out of the jungle, so that they could later be identified. A truly ghastly photograph emerged from Malaya at this time, showing

a Royal Marine commando posing with two decapitated heads; as though
with trophies after a successful hunt. Back in London, an official from
the Colonial Office remarked privately, 'There is no doubt that under
international law, a similar case in wartime would be a war crime'. This
suggests that such officials really did not know that they were fighting
a war.

Having cut off the guerrillas of the MRLA from the food supplies of
their fellow Chinese who were living on the side of the jungle, the British
thought it a good idea to prevent their enemies from producing their own
food. So it was that only eight years after the end of the Second World
War, the British army began using what amounted to chemical warfare
on an industrial scale.

The use of defoliants and herbicides by the American army in Vietnam
was widely condemned during the 1960s and 1970s. The spraying of
toxic chemicals containing dioxin over large areas was injurious not
only to the health of the Vietnamese, but harmed also the soldiers who
were handling the stuff. Most notorious of all the substances used for
this purpose during the Vietnam War was a compound known as Agent
Orange, which contained dioxin. The purpose of the Agent Orange was
to clear huge areas of the jungle in which the Viet-Cong guerrillas had
their bases. This caused an environmental catastrophe though; toxic
chemicals still linger on in the forests of Vietnam, forty years after the
end of the war.

ICI was producing a preparation identical to Agent Orange in the
1950s, called Trioxene. Both Trioxene and Agent Orange had the same
chemical formula; 2,4,5-Trichlorophenoxyacetic acid. Trioxene was sold
as a herbicide and had it not been for the British army in Malaya, it is
altogether possible that nobody would ever have thought for a moment
that what was essentially a powerful weed killer might have any kind
of military application. It was from the British that the Americans
later got the idea of spraying 2,4,5-Trichlorophenoxyacetic acid from
helicopters, in order to destroy many enormous areas of the Vietnamese
jungle.

In 1952, the administration of Malaya bought ICI's entire stock of
Trioxene. At first, this herbicide was sprayed alongside the verges of

roads leading through the jungle. This was to ensure that there was no cover for any guerrillas planning to ambush army patrols. Converted fire engines were used to spread the herbicide. It was found, however, that it was just as easy, and a good deal cheaper, to pay labourers to cut back the vegetation by hand. The vast stockpile of Trioxene would not, however, go to waste.

Now that all the ethnic Chinese who had been living randomly and haphazardly next to the jungle had all been tided away and 'concentrated' in special camps, they were unable to share the crops they produced with the fighters of the MRLA. Controlling food stocks was a key part of the Brigg's Plan. The guerrillas, when not actually engaged in fighting the British, lived in the jungle. It was only natural that they began clearing areas and planting crops of their own. It was these which were now targeted by the army in what was called the, 'Hunger Drive'. The aim was nothing less than to starve their foe into submission.

Now what the British never knew, and the Americans only discovered many years later, was that if 1,3,4-Trichlorophenoxyacetic acid is not produced under very controlled conditions, with the temperature carefully regulated, then heat will cause some of it to degrade, as it is made, into a carcinogenic compound called 2,3,7,8-Tetrachlorodibenzodioxin. In addition to causing cancer, this can cause birth defects, miscarriages, liver damage and various other disorders when long-term exposure takes place. It was this noxious substance which the British began spraying over the crops and camps of the Chinese guerrillas.

General Briggs, who was the head of the British armed forces in Malaya during the early years of the emergency, was very keen to start using Trioxene as soon as possible. In the event, he had been replaced as Director of Operations before the use of the defoliants began against enemy food supplies in March 1953. Although there could hardly be any doubt that this process was a form of chemical warfare, the British decided to bluff it out and dismiss such accusations as 'communist propaganda'. A few weeks after the first helicopters began spraying guerrilla bases and fields, a civil servant in London wrote the following letter, outlining government policy on the matter:

Thank you for your letter of 1 April, with enclosures, about plans for the chemical destruction of terrorist crops in Malaya. We have not discussed the political aspects of this project with the Foreign office, and I do not think it necessary to do so now. It has been common knowledge now for a long time that experiments aimed at destroying terrorist food crops were being carried out, and the rather ridiculous cry of 'chemical warfare' has already been fully exploited in communist propaganda. Whenever it has been raised with us we have been able to give a convincing answer and I do not think there is any need to pursue the point further now.

The destruction of food supplies went on at the same time that a heavy, aerial bombardment was conducted on the jungles of Malaya. From 1950 to 1956, over 14,000 tonnes of bombs were dropped on Malaya; the great majority by bombers of the Royal Australian Air Force. The bombing campaign killed few people, but served to disrupt the guerrilla bases.

We have so far looked at two very different types of concentration camps. The first, those used during the Spanish war in Cuba and the British campaign in South Africa, were used to concentrate entire populations in one place and so prevent them from aiding rebels in any way. The other, for instance the Frongoch concentration camp in Wales, was designed to hold only specific people known, or strongly suspected, to be enemies of the authorities. In Malaya, for the first time, both types of concentration camp were operating and running side by side in tandem. It was this, rather than any efforts to win over the 'hearts and minds' of the populace, which made the British operations in Malaya successful.

At the same time that half a million Chinese peasants were being forcibly evicted from their homes and taken to compounds guarded by the police, the army was also rounding up those whom they suspected of belonging to or supporting the MRLA. Even though there were draconian penalties for helping the guerrillas in any way, the British did not often bother to use the law against those they thought might be working against their interests; they simply locked them, without trial, into prison camps. The man behind this ferocious repression was none other than the originator of the expression, 'hearts and minds'; the new High Commissioner for Malaya, brought in to replace Henry Gurney.

After the assassination of Sir Henry Gurney, the decision was made in London to install a military man who might be able to act decisively to crush the Chinese rebels. General Sir Gerald Templer was a career soldier and veteran of both world wars. He had been commissioned as an officer at the height of the First World War in 1916, when he was only a boy of eighteen. From there, he had worked his way steadily upwards, until being promoted to full general at the age of 52. On 22 January 1952, Prime Minister Winston Churchill appointed Templer as High Commissioner. In order to ensure that he held all the reins of power in his hands and was able to conduct the campaign against the MRLA just as he wanted, Templer took over the post of Director of Operations as well; making him effectively both the ruler and military commander of the country.

During the Iraq War, which began in 2003, and the subsequent occupation; the Americans talked of winning the 'hearts and minds' of the Iraqis. During the Vietnam War, thirty-five years earlier, they had similarly attempted to capture the hearts and minds of the Vietnamese people with, it has to be said, limited success. The first use of the term 'hearts and minds' though was by the newly appointed High Commissioner of Malaya. He gave it as his opinion that military action alone would not be enough to win the struggle against the communist insurgents, saying, 'The answer lies not in pouring more troops into the jungle, but in the hearts and minds of the people'.

As in so many other British colonial possessions, the answer really lay in that old colonial standby of divide and rule. By setting the indigenous Malay people against the Chinese minority, it was hoped to isolate them and emphasise to the Malays that their interests did not coincide with those of their neighbours. Even the relocation of the Chinese squatters into the New Villages tended to reinforce the difference between Malays and Chinese. Many Malay peasants lived in home without electricity and running water and now they saw people without any legal titles to the land upon which they had been living, rewarded with newly built houses with modern facilities. This game that the British had been playing for so many years was a crude one, but exceedingly effective. How else had it been possible to maintain such a mighty empire, for so many years, without the conquered people uniting and rising up against their colonial masters?

For all his talk of 'hearts and minds', the new High Commissioner had made his aim very clear in private conversations, saying that, 'The hard core of armed communists in this country are fanatics and must be, and will be, exterminated'. Believing that the decapitation of dead guerrillas should continue and in fact become a regular practice, Templer approved of the use of Dyak tribesmen from Borneo. The Dyaks were enthusiastic head-hunters and if anybody could be expected to hunt down the enemy and remove their heads neatly and with a minimum of fuss; it was the Dyaks. One problem about using the Dyaks in this way was that the removal of heads was not the only mutilation that they routinely inflicted on the bodies of their enemies. The Colonial office was sufficiently worried about the bad publicity which might result from some of these other habits, that they warned, 'Other practices may have grown up, particularly in units which employ Dyaks, which would provide ugly photographs'. This was putting the case mildly; penises were another of the trophies often collected from corpses.

In addition to the half million or so Chinese men, women and children who were confined behind barbed wire in the New Villages, there was also another type of concentration camp in use in Malaya. Gerald Templer was a great believer in detention without trial; a tactic which the British army had practiced for years, whenever they had the opportunity. During the course of the Malayan Emergency, some 34,000 men were detained without charge in prison camps. Some were held for years, while about 15,000 were deported. The concentration camps in which suspected members of the MRLA were held were similar in many ways to prisoner of war camps. There are no records of any atrocities being committed in these camps. This might perhaps have been because the eyes of the world were, in a sense, focused on South East Asia at this time. The war in Korea, the French struggle for Indo-China; all this meant that newspaper reporters were liable to turn up and ask awkward questions. This was not the case with another colonial war being fought at the same time by the British. In the concentration camps being run in Africa, there were certainly deaths; by hanging, beating and disease. The British gambled on few people being overly concerned about what was being done to black men in an obscure corner of Africa. The savagery in those camps was as bad as anything seen in the twentieth century.

Chapter 9

1952-1960
The Mau Mau Rising: A Million People in Concentration Camps

In previous chapters we have looked at the detention in concentration camps of very large numbers of people at one time. During the South African War at the beginning of the twentieth century, 110,000 Boers were herded into camps and after the Second World War hundreds of thousands of Germans were held in Britain and used as slave labour. Then, in the last chapter, we saw that something in the region of half a million ethnic Chinese were relocated into the 'New Villages', in order to prevent them from offering comfort and aid to the communist insurgents. These numbers pale into insignificance when compared with the camps set up and administered by the British in one African country during the 1950s. By the end of 1955, well over a million men, women and children had been driven from their homes and forcibly resettled in camps surrounded by barbed wire and guarded by watch towers. It was one of the most extensive uses of concentration camps that the world had ever seen.

The Highlands of Kenya, known in colonial times as the 'White Highlands' due to the number of British settlers in the area, contain some of the richest soil in East Africa. The climate is temperate and the growing conditions perfect for coffee. It was perhaps inevitable that the occupying colonial power, the British, should seek to appropriate this desirable land for themselves. This they did over a period of some decades, displacing and virtually enslaving the indigenous inhabitants in the process. The natives were unwillingly transformed from free farmers to wage-slaves, working for white masters. Eventually, the injustice of the colonial system began to cause discontent, which led in time to a rebellion against British rule.

As in so many other parts of the world which they colonised, the British used the time-honoured tactic of divide and rule in Kenya, which was known at one time as the East African Protectorate; before becoming the Kenya Crown Colony. The main tribe in the area was the Kikuyu and it was they who were living in the Highlands which the British settlers coveted. In order to subdue them, the British called on the services of the Masai, who were only to happy to be given the opportunity of massacring those whom they regarded as their historic enemies. In this way, any possible organised opposition to British rule was neutralised and diverted instead into tribal warfare.

During the first half of the twentieth century, some of the Kikuyu left their own country and travelled abroad, where they became politically conscious; returning to Kenya determined to rid themselves of the what they saw as the oppression of British colonialism. One such man was born in the early 1890s and went for the first years of his life by the name of Kamau wa Ngengi. After converting to Christianity, he changed his name to Johnstone Kamau and it was by this name that he was known for many years. In the 1920s, he joined the Kikuyu Central Association; a political group. Representing the KCA, he moved to London, where he became known as Johnstone Kenyatta.

Kenyatta spent almost fifteen years abroad, most of it in England, but including a short spell in Moscow. In 1946, he returned to his own country and began agitating for the rights of the native Africans. In particular, he wished for the land seized by white settlers to be returned to the Kikuyu and also for a timetable to be drawn up for independence. None of this endeared him to the white administration in Kenya. The futile efforts of such people as Kenyatta to achieve peaceful, political change caused some Kikuyu to decide that the only option lay in an armed struggle against those who had stolen their land. This movement, which was known to the whites as Mau Mau, was inspired by men like Kenyatta, who had seen how the world outside Kenya worked and the way in which it was now changing.

Nobody knows the origin of the phrase, 'Mau Mau'. The fighters themselves never used the expression, preferring to refer to themselves as the Kenya Land and Freedom Army or KLFA for short. It was later suggested that 'Mau Mau' was an anagram of 'Uma Uma', which to Kikuyu boys meant simply 'Get out, get out!' and was directed towards the white settlers. Whatever the derivation of the term, the uprising began in earnest on 3 October 1952, with the stabbing to death of a white woman. There had already, for some time, been signs of discontent simmering below the surface and when a chief who was friendly to the British was murdered a few days later, a state of emergency was declared and the Mau Mau uprising began in earnest.

The threat posed by the Kikuyu guerrillas was never as great as the British tried to pretend. By demonising their enemies and making out that a serious rebellion was in progress, the British were able to tighten their hold on the country. The statistics of the conflict provide shocking confirmation of how little threat there really was to the white community. From 1952, when the campaign began, until the end of the emergency in 1960, a total of 12,893 black Africans were killed. In the same period, a mere 107 Europeans died. These figures include both civilians and fighters. The casualty numbers of black fighters and white soldiers are even more astounding. Throughout the whole eight years of the Mau Mau emergency, over 10,500 black guerrillas were killed. Just twelve white soldiers died in action over that same period.

The appalling death toll of Africans and tiny number of white casualties can be accounted for by the weapons being used by the different sides in the conflict. The Mau May fighters were, in the main, armed with machetes, knives, handguns and rifles. The British, on the other hand, had six battalions of well-equipped infantry, artillery and also air power. The RAF in Kenya flew their first mission on 18 November 1953 and were withdrawn on 28 July 1955. In just over eighteen months, the Lincoln bombers in service at that time dropped a devastating six million bombs. Little wonder then at the enormous disparity in casualties!

Military power was one string to the bow of the colonial administration in tackling the uprising. The other was that old standby of the British army overseas; the concentration camp. In Kenya, there were two kinds of concentration camps. On the one hand, those suspected of being involved militarily against the settlers were detained in prison camps. Some 50,000 men, almost all of them Kikuyu, were held in these camps throughout the emergency. The other type of concentration camp was that used in South Africa and Malaya, whereby an entire ethnic group was taken from their homes and held under guard, so that they could not offer aid and comfort to the rebels. Over a million civilians were herded into such places during the Mau Mau uprising.

It was believed that the capital of Kenya, Nairobi, was the centre of the Mau Mau rebellion and so an ambitious security operation was launched to drive any Africans from the city; other than those who were definitely loyal to the white administration. On 24 April 1954, the British army sealed off the African areas of the capital and began the enormous task of arresting every single black person living in Nairobi. The aim of Operation Anvil was to remove every person who might be even suspected of sympathising with the Mau Mau movement. In batches of thousands at a time, black men, women and children were detained and taken to huge compounds, where they were questioned. By the end of the operation, 20,000 men had been identified as probably being Mau Mau supporters and doubts had been raised about a further 30,000.

Because Africans had no more rights in colonial Kenya than they did in South Africa, it was a fairly simple matter to deal effectively with those whom the British suspected of disloyal activities or even attitudes. The 30,000 people about whom there was a question mark were deported to the 'reserves'. These were areas very similar to the Bantustans of apartheid-era South Africa. Well away from the parts of the country where the white settlers lived; many of those sent to the 'reserves' had been born and grown up in Nairobi. This hardly mattered. The main, indeed only, consideration was the safety of the whites.

Even in the reserves, the Kikuyu were not left in peace. Just as in South Africa and Malaya, it was believed that the rebels were being fed and aided by the general population and so even those who were not actively engaged in fighting the British were viewed with suspicion. The solution was the same as that adopted during the Boer War and the Malayan Emergency; to remove the entire suspect population from their homes and keep them under the supervision of the army. Only in this way was it thought, could the supply of food, weapons and information to the rebels be controlled.

A million men, women and children, almost all of them from the Kikuyu tribe, were accordingly removed to barbed wire enclosures, guarded by watchtowers. In some ways, this was similar to the 'New Villages' scheme in Malaya, but with one or two vital differences. The new villages had been designed to offer a higher standard of living than that which the Chinese squatters had previously had, living on the fringe of the jungle. Water and electricity had been laid on for the villages to which they had been moved. In Africa, this was thought to be quite unnecessary. The million or so Kikuyu moved to the guarded camps were expected to build their own homes and were offered little assistance in improving their lives. The primary purpose was to suppress an uprising. There were few newspaper reporters in the African jungle and so there was no need to maintain the pretence, as was done in Malaya, that these deportations were in some way being carried out for the good of the people being herded into captivity.

For ordinary Kikuyu the situation in Kenya was far from attractive, but for those men who were believed to be active members or willing supporters of the Mau Mau; the prospect was grim indeed and remained so for many years. Less than ten years after the end of the Second World War, British troops were involved in setting up concentration camps which reproduced many of the worst features of Belsen and Dachau; from epidemics of typhoid to summary executions and malnutrition. Because these acts of bestiality took place in a corner of a far-off foreign country, a long way from Europe, it was guessed that nobody would object too strenuously; particularly as the victims of the atrocities were all black people.

The system for detaining, interrogating and suppressing men from one particular ethnic group, the Kikuyu, was known as the 'Pipeline'. The aim was to place the prisoners in one of three categories: white, grey or black. Those declared white were those who cooperated with their captors. These men could look forward to being freed and deported to a reserve. The 'greys' were those who had sworn an oath to support Mau Mau. These men often proved susceptible to threats or ill-treatment and some changed sides and joined the British side. Some such men were later employed as guards or interrogators themselves. Then there were the 'blacks'. These were the men who were regarded as the hard core of Mau Mau activists and their fate was to be detained under appalling conditions for as long as was felt to be necessary.

After the screening had taken place and any Kikuyu who could be persuaded to renounce their allegiance to Mau Mau removed, the administration was left with somewhere in the region of 30,000 men who, it was felt, could not be safely freed and sent to the reserves. These were the ones who would be subjected to the most brutal treatment. For instance, the commandants of the concentration camps had complete power of life and death over the prisoners they held. Since the chief object of the exercise was the eradication of the Mau Mau movement, any attempt to get new detainees to join the Mau Mau or pledge their loyalty to the movement was met with a savage response. Those suspected of administering the Mau Mau oath in the camps were publicly hanged in front of the other prisoners. To this day, it is impossible to say how many men were murdered in this way. As far as the British were concerned, any means was justifiable to root out and destroy those planning rebellion against British rule in Kenya.

The camps in which the men who were believed to be active members of the Mau Mau were held had shockingly primitive sanitation; consisting of buckets. These receptacles for the faeces of the prisoners were often left standing alongside the containers of drinking water. It could have come as little surprise to anybody when epidemics of faecal-oral diseases such as typhoid were soon raging in the overcrowded compounds. The health of the prisoners in the Kenyan camps was atrocious and deaths were almost invariably a direct consequence of the conditions in which the men were held. Two camps, Langata and Gilgil, were closed in April 1955 for what were delicately referred to as, 'medical epidemiological' reasons. Because typhoid is a preventable disease, those running the camps sometimes tried to pretend that deaths were from malaria instead; something about which they could have done little. Just as at Belsen, the epidemics of typhoid were a result of overcrowding, poor provision for sanitation and disregard by the guards for the lives of prisoners. The camp of Manyani was a good example of all three processes at work.

Originally designed to accommodate 10,000 men, by September 1954 more than 16,000 were crammed into the compound. The only sanitation consisted of galvanised steel buckets in which the men were required to perform all their bodily functions. Contamination of clean water took place, and an epidemic of typhoid took hold. There were deaths daily from the disease, but sick men were still being forced to work; the guards regarding any claims of illness as malingering. Nobody in Manyani showed any interest in tackling the epidemic, because it affected only prisoners. By the end of the year, there had been 1,151 cases of typhoid at the camp and more than 100 men had died.

Another killer in the concentration camps was pulmonary tuberculosis. This too spread rapidly; due in part to overcrowding but also greatly exacerbated by the fact that many men were suffering from malnutrition and deficiency diseases such as scurvy and kwashiorkor. There was no incentive to deal with these health problems, simply because nobody was in the least worried whether these men lived or died. They were, after all, seen as an intractable problem.

The International Committee of the Red Cross made repeated efforts to gain access to the camps being run by the British army in Kenya, but it was over two years before they were allowed to inspect them. When they finally reached the camps in February 1957, the Red Cross issued a report which detailed the malnutrition and illness that they found. They also raised the question of why the men being detained had not been granted the status of prisoners of war and so accorded the protection of the Geneva Convention.

In addition to deaths from starvation and disease, prisoners were also murdered by the authorities for disobeying the camp rules or even just refusing to work. It was not difficult to present deaths from brutality, starvation or neglect as being due to simple mischance or, a traditional tactic of the British when running their concentration camps, being due to the dirty habits of the prisoners themselves. We saw this being done in both South Africa and Cyprus. One particularly shocking example of this practice will perhaps suffice.

One of the worst of the concentration camps set up in Kenya was that of Hola, in a remote part of the country. Hola held 506 men who were regarded as being extremely uncooperative. Their lack of cooperation was restricted to peaceful protests of the sort advocated by Gandhi. When ordered to pick up spades and set off to work, the men simply sat down and refused to move. The camp commandant was infuriated by this passive resistance and decided that it was his duty to deal with what he chose to see as tantamount to mutiny or rebellion among the prisoners. He issued a number of warnings before matters came to a head on 3 March 1959.

On the morning of Tuesday 3 March 1959, the men being held at Hola were paraded and ordered to pick up spades and picks and get ready to march a mile to the place where they were supposed to be digging an irrigation ditch. The camp Commandant made it perfectly clear that there would be disagreeable consequences for those who disobeyed orders that day. Some of the men decided to comply and set off to work; eighty-eight simply sat down and refused to move.

Sullivan, the Commandant, now put into action a plan which was not of his own devising, but had been formulated and approved by his superiors. The Senior Superintendent of Prisons in Nairobi had visited Hola a few weeks previously and come up with a plan which was to become infamous. If any prisoner refused to obey the order to work then the instructions for the Commandant and his men were written down in black and white: 'It is assumed that the party would obey this order, but if they refused, they would be manhandled to the site of work and forced to carry out the task.' Any normal person reading this instruction would certainly believe that he had been given *carte blanche* to use physical force on the prisoners.

When the order to pick up their tools and start marching to work had been ignored a second time, the order was given to the guards to start beating the recalcitrant prisoners. By the time the guards had finished laying about them with pick-axe handles and other weapons, eleven men had been beaten to death. The reminder were badly injured.

Almost as soon as the massacre had taken place, attempts were made to cover up what had been done. One white man who appeared on the scene a short while later and found eleven corpses laying in a heap, asked what had happened to them. The explanation was not perhaps as plausible as could have been hoped. He was told that the men had been overcome by the heat, had quarrelled and fought and then fainted. Water had been thrown over them to try and revive them, but this had resulted in all of them being drowned! Even in a society used to turning a blind eye to the mistreatment of black Africans, the murders at the Hola Camp were too much. Word leaked out and questions began to be asked in London.

It was still hoped to keep secret what had happened to the men who had been the victims of the massacre in the Hola concentration camp. The official version still involved water, but now it was being claimed that the eleven men had died after drinking contaminated water and had somehow been poisoned by it. It was hinted that their own poor standards of hygiene had contributed to their deaths. Unfortunately for the guilty parties concerned, too many witnesses existed for the matter to be hushed up indefinitely and it was not long before first newspapers and then members of parliament were in full possession of the facts. Within three months, the whole question of the conditions at the Hola camp were being aired in the House of Commons.

It hardly seems possible that the story of the deaths of eleven men from being beaten to death in that way could get any worse and yet so it proved. On 4 June 1959 Sir Barnett Stross, the MP for Stoke-on-Trent, rose in the commons and asked the Secretary of State for the Colonies:

How many of the men who died following the use of physical violence in the Hola camp were suffering from scurvy; and to what extent this deficiency disease contributed to their death.

Scurvy, an extreme and chronic lack of vitamin C, is a consequence of a very poor diet. That the murdered prisoners might have been suffering from malnutrition before their death was shocking indeed. Julian Amery, Under-Secretary of State for the Colonies, was inclined to blame the prisoners themselves for any deficiency diseases that the diet in the concentration camp might have brought about. Not that he was admitting that anybody had been ill. His first reply was that although it was impossible to say if any of the dead men had been suffering from scurvy, 'the evidence suggested that some or all of them may have been suffering from ascorbic acid deficiency at death'. Sir Barnett Stross at once pointed out that ascorbic acid deficiency, or chronic lack of vitamin C, was just another term for scurvy. The Under-Secretary of State went on to explain that men insisted on eating privately in their huts and because of this, it was not always possible to supervise their diet. It was this which had apparently resulted in their developing scurvy!

Eventually, despite the best efforts of the government under Harold Macmillan, the awful truth was revealed about the camps in Kenya. One MP in particular fought hard to prevent the matter being forgotten or suppressed. On 27 July, the Member for Wolverhampton made a rousing and passionate speech on the subjects of the deaths at Hola Camp. His oration was all the more effective for being made by a former Minister of the government then in power; he had been appointed Junior Housing Minister in 1955 and then, in 1957, became Financial Secretary to the Treasury. This rising star of the Conservative party was outraged at the thought that such a dreadful crime might be brushed under the carpet or made light of. He said in his speech:

> *We cannot say 'We will have African standards in Africa, Asian standards in Asia and perhaps British standards here at home.' We have not that choice to make. We must be consistent with ourselves everywhere. All government, all influence of man upon man, rests on opinion. What we can do in Africa, where we can still govern and where we no longer govern, depends upon the opinion which is entertained of the way in which this country acts and the way in which Englishmen act. We cannot, we dare not, in Africa of all places, fall below our own highest standards in the acceptance of responsibility.*

This speech was widely thought to have been a masterpiece of parliamentary rhetoric. Ironically, the orator was none other than Enoch Powell, who later went on to epitomize racial prejudice and intolerance.

Eventually, it became clear to the government that action would need to be taken against those responsible for the massacre at the Hola camp. It proved to be the mildest of rebukes, with two senior officials compelled to retire early. They were not however deprived of their pensions.

Times were changing and this was acknowledged even by the Prime Minister himself. A little less than a year after the Hola massacre, Harold Macmillan visited British colonial possessions in Africa and then went on to South Africa, where he gave a speech which referred to the 'Wind of change'. Addressing the South African parliament in Cape Town, he said that; 'The wind of change is blowing through this continent. Whether we like it or not, this growth of national consciousness is a political fact.' Although the Conservatives had, throughout the 1950s tried to hang on to colonies such as Kenya and the Gold Coast, it was clear by 1960 that this was not possible. The methods used in Kenya to retain control of the country had shown that only by imitating the Nazis would it be practical to continue ruling parts of Africa. The idea of using concentration camps and murdering those offering passive resistance to the British administration was too much to stomach at the beginning of the new decade.

Kenya gained its independence in 1963 and it seemed that Britain's use of the concentration camp as a tool of political power had finally come to an end. There was though to be one more brief and unsavoury sequence of events in the British love affair with punitive camps and it took place a good deal closer to home than East Africa. This final use of concentration camps was, unusually, described as such by a British Home Secretary as, for the first time since the end of the Second World War, it was openly admitted that a concentration camp was being maintained and administered by the British government. What made this all the more shocking was that the establishment in question was running for years not in Malaya, Cyprus or Africa, but actually within the United Kingdom itself.

Chapter 10

1971-1975
Operation Demetrious and the Five Techniques: The Detention and Torture of Political prisoners in Northern Ireland

On 9 November 2005, Tony Blair's government suffered its first ever defeat in the House of Commons. It was a momentous occasion, prompting rumours that the Prime Minister might resign. It is, after all, not often that a government with such a strong majority is defeated on a matter of major policy. The Labour Party discovered that on some issues, even its own MPs would not toe the party line. What was the subject of this humiliating setback for one of the government's most cherished policies? It was the idea that those suspected of terrorist offences might be detained for up to ninety days without being charged or brought before a court. After the rebellion, this figure was reduced to twenty-eight days; although many felt that that too was unacceptably long to hold a person who had not been charged with, let alone convicted of, any crime.

The debate which seemed to be of such great importance in 2005, the haggling over whether terrorist suspects should be held for fourteen, twenty-eight or ninety days without charge, had a slightly unreal air about it for anybody over the age of forty or so. It was, after all, only thirty years since suspected terrorists could be detained without charge in the United Kingdom not for two weeks, four weeks or a couple of months; but literally indefinitely. In 1975, just three decades before the debate which caused such anguish to so many Labour MPs, a Labour government was keeping prisoners behind barbed wire who had been locked up without charge for over four years! Nor was this all. Some of these prisoners had been subjected to the most brutal treatment; treatment which by any definition, and even on the admission of the man who had been Home Secretary at the time, amounted to torture.

We are regularly regaled in the newspapers and other mass media with accounts of the horrific treatment meted out to suspected terrorists by the CIA; the illegal arrests and deportations known as extraordinary rendition, torture in various unofficial prisons and of course detention at the special camp at Guantanamo Bay in Cuba. The slightest hint that Britain might perhaps have been cooperating with these dubious activities, or indeed to have been involved in any way, however peripheral, is greeted with shocked amazement and demands for an enquiry. It is little short of astounding to hear such cries of outrage, when we remember how the British themselves were engaging in exactly the same, unsavoury practises during the 1970s.

Just over 700 prisoners have passed through the American camp at their naval base at Guantanamo Bay. Hardly any of these men have been charged with any offence; the vast majority being detained because they are suspected by the American Secret Service of terrorist activity. By comparison, 2,000 prisoners were held without charge at the Long Kesh Camp in Northern Ireland and other centres for political prisoners. None of these men were ever charged with any offence and some were kept as prisoners for over four years. A number were tortured by British troops while being detained. This is not incidentally the view of some biased newspaper; in 1976 the European Commission for Human Rights ruled that political prisoners being held without trial in Northern Ireland had indeed been tortured during their interrogation.

The widespread detention and torture of political prisoners in the United Kingdom seems sometimes to have slipped from the memory of most people living in that country. That hundreds of men were being held behind barbed wire for years at a time, with no prospect of being charged or released sounds like some Kafkaesque vision, but the last such detainees were released as recently as Christmas, 1975.

The British have a genius for euphemism. Most countries have a Minister for the Interior; the British equivalent is the cosy-sounding Home Secretary. Only the British could describe a state of armed conflict lasting for thirty years, and all but indistinguishable at times from civil war, as 'The Troubles'. When 'The Troubles' began in 1969, it must for the first year or two have seemed like just one more of the the periodic outbreaks of violence organised by Irish nationalists. From the Easter Rising of 1916 onwards, there had been sporadic campaigns of terrorism and outbreaks of disorder which affected both Ireland itself and also mainland Britain.

In 1920, there was the great 'IRA Scare'; squads of Irish terrorists who came to the mainland for the sole purpose of starting an arson campaign which was designed to harm England economically. In 1922, Sir Henry Wilson, an important military figure, was assassinated by the IRA in London. In 1939, a ferocious bombing campaign was launched by the IRA against the British mainland. Explosions took place in London and various other cities; culminating in August 1939 with a bomb attack in the Midlands city of Coventry, which killed five people. From 1956 to 1962, a campaign of guerrilla warfare began in Northern Ireland, which became known as the 'Border Campaign'. A number of bombings and shootings were carried out during this time by the IRA. So when, seven years after the end of the Border Campaign, the IRA once again began to posture and threaten, there was no reason at first to regard it as more than another of the occasional, low-level actions which had plagued Britain and Northern Ireland since the end of the First World War.

The British government, together with the administration in Northern Ireland, had a sovereign remedy for these ills; a ready solution to any kind of terrorism involving the IRA. It was called the *1922 Special Powers Act* and it enabled the government of Northern Ireland to deal with any disorder or violence by locking people up without the inconvenience of a trial for as long as they pleased. First introduced in 1922, as a response to the Irish Civil War, the Special Powers Act was made permanent in 1933, which meant that well into the 1970s, political power in Northern Ireland was ultimately backed by a piece of emergency legislation passed only a few years after the end of the First World War.

The Special Powers Act or, to give it its full name, *The Civil Authorities (Special Powers) Act (Northern Ireland) 1922*, was for over forty years the way that political power was ultimately enforced in part of the United

Kingdom. It authorised the Minister of Home Affairs in the government of Northern Ireland to, 'take all such steps and issue all such orders as may be necessary for preserving peace and maintaining order'. In short, the minister could do *literally* anything at all that he felt was necessary to maintain order. Not only did it provide for the setting up of concentration camps for political prisoners, it also made provision for the burning down and blowing up of people's homes and the instituting of curfews; to say nothing of flogging those taking part in demonstrations or owning a car. The Act was in force until the middle of the 1970s. Here are some of the things covered by the Special Powers Act:

1. The civil authority may by order require every person within any area specified in the order to remain within doors between such hours as may be specified in the order

3. (1) The civil authority may make orders prohibiting or restricting in any area:
(e) The having, keeping or using of a motor or other cycle, or motor car by any person, other than a member of the police force, without a permit from the civil authority

8. It shall be lawful for the civil authority and any person duly authorised by him, where for the purposes of this Act it is necessary so to do:
(d) To cause any buildings or structures to be destroyed

26. The civil authority may by notice prohibit the circulation of any newspaper for any specified period

There is something utterly chilling about the fact that for half a century, part of the United Kingdom was under such a draconian law. It was this same Act which authorised the detention without trial of anybody for any length of time. Not only that, but:

5. Where after trial by any court a person is convicted of any crime or offence to which this section applies, the court may, in addition to

any other punishment which may be lawfully imposed, order such a
person, if male, to be once privately whipped

In other words, those breaking a curfew or owning a car without the permission of the authorities could be flogged for it and possibly have their home demolished into the bargain.

So much for the text of this astonishing piece of legislation. Perhaps though it was one of those bits of law which was seldom actually invoked? In other words, just something which found its way onto the Statute Book during an emergency and by some oversight, was somehow was never replaced or abolished. History tells us a different story. The concentration camp was, for the first fifty years or so of Northern Ireland's existence, an integral part of its judicial system.

Following the partition of Ireland in 1921 into the Free State of the south and the province of Northern Ireland in the north, there was a lot of violence across the whole of Ireland. In the south, this resulted in a civil war, but in the north, a consequence of the rioting and disorder was the passing of the Special Powers Act. It was used at once to deal with the troublesome Catholic minority of the new province. In May 1922, 300 men were arrested and kept in custody for the next two years, without any charges. This proved to be such an effective way of dealing with political opposition, that sixteen years later, the same tactic was adopted. On 22 December 1938, internment was used again in Northern Ireland, when thirty-four men were arrested as a result of conspiracy which had supposedly been uncovered by the government in Belfast.

Internment was the term used in Northern Ireland for imprisonment without trial. It was used on both sides of the border; the government of the Irish Free State, later the Irish Republic, being no keener on the IRA than their counterparts in the north. In 1922 and then again in 1940, the Irish government cooperated in a sense with Northern Ireland to suppress IRA activity. The men picked up and interned in Northern Ireland in 1938 were destined to spend a considerable length of time being held without trial. In fact some of them were not released until the end of the war in 1945. Just to make this perfectly clear, British citizens were being arrested in part of the United Kingdom and then held for seven years without being brought before a court or even charged with any offence.

The last of the internees were freed in 1945, but only eleven years later, internment was once more being used on both sides of the border. On 11 December 1956, there was a series of explosions at targets on the border between the Irish Republic and the north. Less than two weeks later, internment was used to detain 400 men who were suspected by the Royal Ulster Constabulary of being involved in terrorist activity. Of these men, 167 were still being held without charge six years later, when the IRA campaign finally petered to a halt in 1962. Once again, internment was also used on the other side of the border, which meant in effect that the IRA leadership had no hiding place.

By the middle of the 1960s, many Catholics in Northern Ireland were dissatisfied with the conditions under which they were living and determined to force political change. Living standards in the province were lower than in the rest of the United Kingdom and Catholic standards of living there were lower than those of the Protestant majority. This inequality was maintained by a corrupt and enormously unfair political system. Having seen civil rights movements in the United States which were demanding equal electoral rights for blacks in the the southern states, under the slogan of 'One man, one vote', it came as something of a shock for the British to find that this same cry was being raised in part of their own country!

As a matter of fact, the electoral system in Northern Ireland was grotesquely unfair to the Catholic minority. For one thing, there were property qualifications for voting in local elections; something which favoured Protestants, who were more likely to be home owners. Even worse, there was plural voting; those who owned businesses were entitled to extra votes. All of which helped ensured that the more wealthy Protestant community remained in power. In 1967, an organisation called the Northern Ireland Civil Rights Association was founded and this group soon began to organise marches and protests, with a view to ensuring that there was indeed, 'One man, one vote' in the province.

For the next two years, things grew increasingly tense in Northern Ireland, with the hardline Protestant government reluctant to relinquish any of the power which they had held since the setting up of the province in 1921. Then, in 1969, events began spiralling out of control. In March and April, there were bomb attacks on power stations and waterworks. Also in April, there was serious rioting in the Bogside district of Londonderry. One or two people died as a result of these disturbances. The police response to marches and demonstrations was often to attack those taking part, almost invariably Catholics, and disperse them with baton charges.

Behind the scenes, preparations were being made for the most momentous intervention by the government in London into the affairs of Northern Ireland for many years. On 2 August 1969, there were more riots in Belfast and the RUC found that they were barely able to control the violence, which was threatening to spread across the whole city. The next day, sixty soldiers were despatched to Belfast, where they were accommodated in a police barracks. Some troops were also moved to Londonderry. It was becoming increasingly obvious that the regular police, even supported by the special constabulary, would not be able to cope much longer.

As the 'Marching Season' began, the violence on the streets escalated, with protests and counter protests taking place throughout August. From 13 August to 15 August 1969, the so-called 'Battle of the Bogside' raged in Londonderry, with Catholics and Protestants battling for control of the streets. On the afternoon of 14 August 1969, the first British soldiers appeared on the streets of Northern Ireland. Their role was essentially to separate the warring factions in Londonderry and prevent the violence from escalating.

In Belfast, the situation was even worse. First petrol bombs and then hand grenades were thrown at police vehicles. On 14 August, shots began to be exchanged between the RUC and the crowds and houses were set on fire. In a breathtaking over-reaction, the police brought in armoured cars with heavy machine guns and began firing more or less randomly at blocks of flats in a Catholic area.

By the early hours of 15 August, gun battles were raging between the police and IRA gunmen. At the same time, Catholic refugees were fleeing their homes, which were then being put to the torch by Protestant mobs. The situation was deteriorating into something approaching civil war. At

4:30 am, the Police Commissioner for Belfast asked for military aid. By this time, the RUC had withdrawn to their bases, in order to defend them; leaving the streets to the rival crowds of rioters and gunmen. At 12:25 that afternoon, the cabinet of the Northern Ireland government appealed to the Home Secretary in London for troops to be sent to maintain order. Later that day men of the Royal Regiment of Wales began patrolling the Falls Road as part of peacekeeping duties. At the time, it was assumed that this would be a temporary measure, lasting perhaps for a week or two.

For the next two years, the British army became ever more deeply embroiled in the affairs of Northern Ireland. The old IRA leadership, those who had been involved in the Border Campaign of 1956-1962 or even the 1939 bombing campaign, had shown themselves unable to adapt to the new, fast-moving situation which had erupted in Northern Ireland. In December 1969, a new movement emerged in the course of a schism within the IRA. This was the Provisional IRA and they saw their enemy to be not just the Protestant government of the province and the RUC, but also the British army, who were now patrolling the streets of Belfast and Londonderry. The army found themselves not so much keeping the peace between two warring communities, but rather locked in a guerrilla war with republican paramilitaries.

For the British army, the situation in which they were involved after the summer of 1969 was both unexpected and unwelcome. Troops had been deployed on the streets of Northern Ireland before for peacekeeping duties, in 1935, but on that occasion as soon as the violence had subsided, the soldiers returned to the mainland. It was at first envisaged that much the same thing would happen in 1969. After the first troops had been sent onto the streets of Londonderry, a civil servant in Whitehall predicted that they would be back in their barracks by the weekend. In the event, it was to be over thirty years before the army returned to its barracks and were no longer visible on the streets of Northern Ireland's towns and cities.

The resurgent IRA began during 1970 to take ever more aggressive actions; initially against the commercial life of the province and then later targeting the army directly. The first bombs were detonated in 1970 and throughout that year, the Provisional IRA became more confident and started to represent themselves as protecting Catholic civilians against the excesses of the British army. In June, 1970, the Labour government of Harold Wilson was replaced by a Conservative administration led by Edward Heath. The new government evidently proposed to take a tough line on the violence in Northern Ireland from the start.

Within a matter of weeks of coming to power, Heath's government decided that the simmering discontent in Northern Ireland could be suppressed by a show of firmness. They believed that the previous administration had been pussy-footing around and that this had only made the IRA bolder. The new Home Secretary, Reginald Maudling, passed an extremely tought new piece of legislation called the Criminal Justice (Temporary Provisions) Act. This made mandatory a six-month prison sentence for those convicted of rioting. Since the only people capable of arresting those suspected of this offence were the army, it did nothing to increase the popularity of the thousands of troops who were now stationed in the province. The resentment felt about protesters who were taken off by the army and then sent to prison for six months strengthened the position of the Provisional IRA.

Up until now, the army's role had essentially been reactive; they dealt with trouble as and when it arose. Now, they were ordered to go on the offensive. On 3 July 1970, a number of raids were made in Catholic areas. The army's intention was to seek out the IRA arms dumps that they knew to be in and around the Falls Road district of Belfast. In one sense, the operation was a great success; a total of thirty rifles, fifty-two pistols and twenty-four shotguns were seized. Unfortunately, while breaking down doors and searching people's homes, a good deal of damage was done and local residents began a protest which swiftly turned into a riot. At first, large amounts of CS tear gas were fired at the crowds, but when this failed to do the trick; the army declared a curfew, which was maintained for thirty-six hours. Anybody venturing out of their house was promptly arrested. It need hardly be said that none of this exactly endeared the British troops to the Catholic residents of Belfast and it proved in fact to be the biggest recruiting boost that the IRA had yet received since the Troubles had begun the previous year.

Things were rapidly going from bad to worse and the tougher the actions of the soldiers, the greater the number of new fighters recruited into the Provisonal IRA. On 6 February 1971, came the first murder of a British soldier in Northern Ireland. Robert Curtis was a gunner with the Royal Artillery and arrived in Northern Ireland with his regiment at the beginning January 1971. On 6 February, he was dealing with a disturbance in Belfast, when a burst of automatic fire cut him down. He was twenty years of age. The following month, three Scottish soldiers, the youngest of whom was just seventeen, were lured to their deaths and murdered.

It was becoming apparent that some dramatic action might be needed to put an end to the mounting violence and disorder in the province. It was now eighteen months since the army had first been deployed and so far, every new development saw a deterioration in the situation. There appeared to be two main options; neither of which was especially attractive, but one of which was thought to be considerably worse than the other. The first possibility would be to use the army in an aggressive role, in effect waging war against the IRA and using any methods possible to destroy the terrorist group. This had the potential to turn into a catastrophic public relations disaster for Britain and there was little appetite in London for this particular course of action. The second option was one being eagerly pushed by the Protestant leaders of Northern Ireland. Previous outbreaks of IRA activity had been nipped in the bud by the judicious use of internment without trial, as provided for in the Special Powers Act. Surely, it was now time to give this a try?

The Northern Ireland government in Belfast might have been keen to see the reintroduction of internment in the province, but their enthusiasm was not shared by the army. Senior officers could see what the politicians apparently could not; that arresting people without warrants and then depositing them in concentration camps was likely to provoke an unprecedented storm of anger among the Catholics and their self-appointed defenders, the Provisional IRA. Since any move in this direction would need the army to carry out the arrests and then cope with any resulting flare-up of terrorism and civil disorder, the ultimate decision on the matter was left not to the Protestant administration at the Stormont parliament building in Belfast, but rather with the British government at Westminster. Defence Secretary Lord Carrington was greatly in favour of the scheme and so too was the Leader of the House of Commons, William Whitelaw. Prime Minister Edward Heath was persuaded that internment was the only way that the rising tide of violence could be stemmed and so he gave his consent for the use of detention without trial.

One obstacle at once presented itself; in 1971 was that there simply was not enough room in the prisons of Northern Ireland for hundreds of extra prisoners. Northern Ireland had at that time one of the lowest rates of imprisonment in the whole of Europe. There were only 700 prisoners in the province and since the initial planning being made was to arrest around 400 suspects, this would have increased the number of prison places needed by over 50 per cent. The solution which was found was neat and utterly disastrous for Britain's image abroad.

About 15km from Belfast, not far from the town of Lisburn was, during the Second World War, an RAF base called Long Kesh. Although of some importance during the war, the 360 acre site had been more or less disused since 1945. What Long Kesh did have though was a stout perimeter fence and also rows of corrugated-iron Nissen huts, which had formerly been used as barracks for the RAF personnel from the base. It seemingly escaped the notice of those laying plans for the use of internment without trial that Long Kesh looked like nothing so much as a concentration camp; which of course was precisely what it was to become. Long Kesh was not the only site chosen for imprisoning the dissidents and terrorists whom the army would shortly be rounding up. In an uncomfortable echo of the prison hulks which featured in Dickens' novel *Great Expectations*, a former submarine depot ship of the Royal Navy, HMS *Maidstone*, was moored at Belfast and used as a prison ship.

At 4:30 am on 9 August 1971, the army went into action; 'lifting' 342 men from across the province. Somehow, word had leaked out about the projected raids and quite a few of those for whom the troops were searching had had time to slip across the border into the Irish Republic. The lists which had been prepared by the politicians and police in Northern Ireland were hopelessly out-of-date and a number of those detained had had no involvement with the IRA since the 1939 bombing campaign.

That this was the case may be seen by looking at the aftermath of the raids. Of the 342 men arrested, a third, 116 men, were released within forty-eight hours. These were men who had no connection at all with either terrorism or any other subversive activity.

The army showed themselves considerably more prescient about the situation in Northern Ireland than did the politicians who had lived there all their lives. Just as senior officers had predicted, the use of the Special Powers Act in this way caused a huge and immediate surge of violence. In the four months before the introduction of internment, four soldiers and four civilians had died throughout the province. This was the level of violence which was thought to be severe enough to call for the suspension of *habeus corpus*. In the four months following the arrests on 9 August, thirty soldiers, eleven police officers and no fewer than seventy-three civilians were killed. Rather than damping down the crisis in Northern Ireland, the use of detention without trial had had the effect of throwing petrol on a smouldering fire.

The introduction of internment without trial was called by the army Operation Demetrius. Arresting the suspects was only the first stage in the process. Most of those who had not been released would end up in the camp at Long Kesh, on the prison ship or in another base near Londonderry. For fourteeen men though, being arrested arbitrarily in this way and held without charge was the beginning of a nightmare. The army were under orders from London to track down the leaders of the insurgency in Northern Ireland and the way that they were to accomplish this task was by the use of torture. For many years, it was assumed that the torturing of the IRA suspects seized in 1971 had been a piece of private enterprise on the part of junior officers; men who had become a little over-enthusiastic about the interrogation of suspects. It was not until many years later that it came to light that these men were, far from acting on their own initiative, obeying orders from the very top of the command chain.

Even before the news leaked out of the systematic torture of selected prisoners, those released forty-eight hours after being arrested had disturbing tales to tell. Some had allegedly been forced to run the gauntlet between rows of soldiers who were swinging batons at them.

Others had been taken into helicopters while blindfolded and then, after the helicopters had taken off and been flying for a while, were told that they were hundreds of feet in the air. They were then thrown out of the open door of the helicopter. Only when they landed with a bump, a second later, did they discover that the helicopter had only been hovering a few feet above the ground.

The stories related by the men who had been arrested and then freed, were so similar that it was unlikely that they were simply inventions. The British army were experimenting with fairly crude techniques to break the spirits of their prisoners. Although the methods used on many of the men who had been picked up with a view to interning them were little more than playful cruelty, more sophisticated ways of interrogation were ready to be used. These were known as the 'Five Techniques' and they represented the culmination of the army's experience around the world, throughout the twentieth century, in extracting information from those who were reluctant to part with it. Fourteen men were subjected to these methods of obtaining information.

The prisoners who were felt to be in possession of valuable information were flown to the former RAF base of Ballykelly; which, since 2 June 1971, had functioned as an army barracks. A special interrogation centre had been set up at Ballykelly and the idea was that by quickly getting as much information from the men taken there, the army might be able to put an end to the activities of the Provisional IRA once and for all. In defence of the army, it must be remembered that at this stage of The Troubles, it was still thought that with a little firm action, the civil unrest could be nipped in the bud. It was this frame of mind which led to the next stage of Operation Demetrious.

We must remind ourselves that the men who had been arrested by the army and taken to Ballykelly had not been detained for any specific offence. Nor were they to be charged or brought before a court. These men had been picked up with a view to holding them indefinitely in a concentration camp, but first they were to be tortured. This is not, incidentally, a snap judgement on the part of the author, but rather the verdict of the European Commission on Human Rights in 1976. To be fair, two years later, they revised their opinion and stated that perhaps what was done to the internees amounted not to torture, but merely to 'inhuman and degrading treatment'.

What were the 'Five Techniques' used over the course of a week on those being questioned? They were the withholding of food and drink, deprivation of sleep, prolonged exposure to noise, hooding and being made to stand against a wall for long periods of time. Together, these methods produced disorientation and confusion in all who were subjected to them. The men were kept handcuffed and their heads covered with hoods, while being kept in cold cells, where they were subjected to so-called 'white noise'; a loud hissing which drowned out all other sound. This sensory deprivation made it impossible for them to keep track of time and they did not know if it was day or night. They were forced, while still hooded, to stand against walls in a stressful and uncomfortable position; with their arms stretched above their heads and leaning forward against the wall. Those who collapsed were beaten and forced to resume the position. While this was going on, it was of course impossible to sleep and they were offered nothing to eat or drink.

The result of this treatment was that the men began to suffer from hallucinations and to lose consciousness. While this was going on, their heads were sometimes banged against the wall and they were threatened with even more severe mistreatment if they did not cooperate with the interrogators.

Word leaked out about what was being done to these interned prisoners and the British government appointed Sir Edmund Compton, a distinguished civil servant, to investigate the claims being made in newspapers about what had been going on in Ballykelly. Although the language he used was balanced and appeared to bend over backwards to avoid suggesting that the security forces in Northern Ireland had been guilty of torture; the report of the Compton Committee, which was published on 16 November 1971, infuriated Prime Minister Edward Heath.

Before seeing what Edward Heath had to say, we might look at a passage from the report which explained away the brutality used during the interrogations and indeed explained why there had in fact not been any brutal behaviour at all. Sir Edmund's explanation is a masterpiece:

Where we have concluded that physical ill-treatment took place, we are not making a finding of brutality on the part of those who handled these complainants. We consider that brutality is an inhuman or savage form of cruelty, and that cruelty implies a disposition to inflict suffering, coupled with indifference to, or pleasure in, the victim's pain. We do not think that happened here.

In other words, the Compton Committee decided that because the soldiers had not enjoyed what they were doing, it was impossible for their actions to be brutal! This stunning piece of sophistry, which effectively exculpated any of the staff at Ballykelly interrogation centre from the charge of brutality or cruelty, struck some people as bizarre.

Despite doing their best to describe the treatment of those who became known as the 'hooded men' as 'physical ill-treatment' and not torture, Edward Heath was disgusted by what he saw as support for the IRA against the army. He wrote in a memo, 'It seems to me one of the most unbalanced, ill-judged reports I have ever read.' The memo, which came to light shortly before Heath's death in 2005, continued, 'When you go through the report carefully, the number of incidents involved in the arrest of 300 odd men were small.' Which meant that since only fourteen out of 300 or so were tortured, this could perhaps be disregarded. It is plain that the Prime Minister was absolutely livid about the report and felt that it was an attack on the army:

Here they seem to have gone to endless lengths to show that anyone not given 3-star hotel facilities suffered hardship and ill-treatment. Again, nowhere is this set in the context of war against the IRA.

It was to be forty years before the truth about the torture used on the men arrested and interned was to come to light. In the course of a television programme about the interrogation techniques used, the RTE television station in the Republic of Ireland came across some correspondence between former Home Secretary Merlyn Rees and then Prime Minister James Callaghan. In a documentary broadcast in 2014, a letter sent by Rees in 1977 was revealed, which contained the following passage:

It is my view (confirmed by Brian Faulkner before his death) that the
decision to use methods of torture in Northern Ireland in 1971/72 was
taken by Ministers – in particular Lord Carrington, then Secretary
of State for Defence.

In other words, not only was it admitted that torture *had* been used, but
it was sanctioned by the government in London and was not some action
undertaken by maverick army officers on their own initiative.

Meanwhile, for the majority of prisoners, those who had not been
tortured; life went on. The conditions of their confinement were
monotonous and boring, but could have been a good deal worse. In
fact, whatever the official line being taken, the IRA men picked up for
internment were treated as prisoners of war.

The prison camp at Long Kesh was divided into 'cages'. These were
barbed wire enclosures, each of which held four Nissen huts. Three were
for the prisoners to sleep in and the fourth to be used as a canteen.
Each hut, measuring about 120 by 24 feet, housed forty prisoners. In
British prisons at that time, inmates were compelled to wear a distinctive
uniform. Internees were spared this indignity and could wear their own
clothes. There was completely free association and the prison guards
would pass all instructions through the senior officers of the IRA. Food
parcels were allowed and the men spent their days in attending lectures
on politics and military tactics. They even drilled with wooden guns.
Like prisoners of war, the internees also believed strongly that they had a
duty to escape. This led to a most extraordinary episode in January 1972,
when seven of the men being held prisoner did indeed escape; much to
the embarrassment of both the army and the British government.

HMS *Maidstone*, moored at the coal wharf in Belfast docks, held 122
of the men who had been interned in August 1971. The conditions on
the ship were cramped and unsanitary; with little room for exercise.
Following the principle that that they were duty-bound to escape if
they could, a group of the Republicans being held on HMS *Maidstone*
decided to try and swim to freedom. It would be impossible to get off
the ship via the gangplank, because this was heavily guarded by troops.
Diving into the water of the harbour looked as though it might be a

fairly straightforward enterprise, but coils of barbed wire just below the surface gave the impression that they would then be unable to get any further. One day though, it was noticed that a seal had managed to swim through the barbed wire and this suggested that it might perhaps be possible for men too to squeeze through the barbed wire, thus allowing them to swim ashore.

On the night of 17 January 1972, seven men sawed through a steel bar fixed across a porthole and then slid down the steel cables into the icy water. Their names were Jim Bryson, Tommy Tolan, Thomas Kane, Martin Taylor, Tommy Gorman, Peter Rodgers and Sean Convery. The escape had been delayed for twenty minutes, due to an unexpected headcount by the guards. The men were almost naked and had smeared their bodies with butter to insulate themselves against the freezing temperatures. They had also rubbed boot polish over their skin so that they would not be so visible in the dark waters of the harbour.

Getting through the tangles of barbed wire that were suspended in the water proved a lot more difficult for the escaping prisoners than they had believed might be the case. Several men were badly lacerated as they struggled through. Things were made even more arduous, due to the fact that not all of the seven could swim. Arrangements had been made with the IRA in Belfast that they would be waiting for the escapees with transport and warm clothing. Unfortunately, due both to the late start to the escape and also the surprisingly long time that it took for them to swim to the rendezvous point, the men who had been planning to meet them came to the conclusion that the escape had been called off. They went home before the seven escapees reached the harbour side. The men from the prison ship clambered ashore, dripping wet and freezing cold; dressed only in their underpants.

After managing to hijack a bus, the seven men from HMS *Maidstone* drove across Belfast to a Republican enclave. They were spotted en route by an army patrol who, intrigued by the sight of seven almost naked men racing along in a corporation bus, gave chase. When the bus reached the Markets area though, the army decided not to pursue it further, lest they ended up being ambushed. The men were then spirited away and later smuggled across the border into the Irish Republic. They later gave a press conference in Dublin. This revealed a fatal flaw in the use of internment by the government of Northern Ireland and gave a strong clue as to why it was not as effective in the 1970s as it had been during previous campaigns against the IRA.

In 1939 and again in 1956, the implementation of the 1922 Special Powers Act in the north was mirrored by the use of internment in the south. In other words, wanted IRA men knew that even if they managed to elude the police in Northern Ireland and were able to slip south across the border; they were still at risk of being picked up and held without trial. It was this which had made internment so effective previously. Now though, the case was quite different. The government of the Irish Republic viewed what had been happening to the Catholics in the north as virtually amounting to a pogrom. They had not the slightest intention of coordinating their legal system with that of the Protestant dominated north and assisting them by picking up wanted IRA fugitives and either holding them without trial in the south or handing them back across the border. This meant in practice that the south was a safe haven for those wanted by the police or army in Northern Ireland.

The numbers of internees fluctuated, but until the summer of 1972 remained at around the 250 mark. Events in that first year of the United Kingdom's last experiment with the holding of political prisoners was to increase that number dramatically.

Far from quelling the unrest, as was hoped, internment served only to fan the flames. Gun battles between terrorists and the security forces became a regular feature of life in the province. In January 1972 came one of the worst incidents of The Troubles: the massacre of fourteen unarmed men by soldiers of the paratroops; a unit renowned for ruthlessness in combat and perhaps not the best men to use for a peacekeeping operation. Following what became known as 'Bloody Sunday', the situation in Northern Ireland deteriorated still further, until by March what was a civil war, in all but name, was raging. The violence was not confined to Northern Ireland, which made things even more alarming for the government in London. Two days after 'Bloody Sunday', the British Embassy in Dublin was burned to the ground. Then, on 22 February, a car bomb exploded at the headquarters of the Parachute Regiment in the English town of Aldershot, killing seven people, including a Catholic priest.

It was clear that the government of Northern Ireland was quite unable, even with military assistance from London, to maintain order and stability and that the bloodshed in the province was likely to proliferate in other parts of the British Isles. It was against this background that the British government decided to take over the direct running of Northern Ireland; dissolving the assembly which had been running the province since 1922. On 30 March 1972, the *Northern Ireland (Temporary Provisions) Act 1972* received Royal Assent. It is a matter of common observation that nothing lasts like the temporary; it was to be another thirty years or so before the government of Northern Ireland was handed back to its citizens.

William Whitelaw was appointed the first Secretary of State for Northern Ireland and immediately faced a legal problem. The assumption of rule from Westminster meant that various pieces of legislation relating to Northern Ireland were automatically set aside. One of these was the *Special Powers Act of 1922*. This meant that the legal basis for the detention of the interned prisoners being held in the camp at Long Kesh and the prison ship, HMS *Maidstone*, was null and void. This in turn would mean either releasing the prisoners at once or rushing through an enabling law. The Detention of Terrorists (N.I.) Order 1942 (1972 No. 1632 [N.I.15]), which was made under the provisions of the Northern Ireland (Temporary Provisions) Act, dealt with this little difficulty and ensured that the government could continue to hold suspects for the rest of their lives if necessary.

By the end of July 1972, the number of prisoners being held without trial in Northern Ireland had fallen to 243. This was to change on the last day of that month. Since 1971, the IRA had established so-called 'No-Go Areas' in Belfast and Londonderry. Barricades had been erected and strengthened until even the armoured vehicles used by the British army were not powerful enough to break through them. Within these parts of the cities, the IRA operated at will; manning roadblocks, administering their own brand of justice and doing exactly as they wished. No police or troops could enter these zones.

Using the No-Go Areas as bases, the Provisional IRA launched increasingly ferocious terrorist attacks across the whole of the province. On 21 July 1972, the IRA detonated twenty-two bombs in Belfast over the space of an hour and a quarter. Nine civilians and two soldiers were killed and 130 other people injured. Clearly, the situation was once again growing intolerable and it was the army which would be called upon to deal with things.

In the biggest military operation carried out by the British army since the invasion of Suez in 1956, 22,000 soldiers, backed by tanks, launched an assault on the No-Go Areas. They were re-taken and the rule of the IRA ended. There was however a sharp rise in the number of men captured by the army and then interned.

For the next three years, hundreds of prisoners languished in the prison camp of Long Kesh; having no prospect at all of either being brought to trial or released. They existed in a legal limbo; technically innocent, but subjected to administrative detention. It was a state of affairs which attracted worldwide condemnation for the British government and it was not until the General Election of February 1974 that there was any possibility of the situation being resolved.

When the Labour leader Harold Wilson was invited by the Queen to form a minority government at the beginning of March 1974, he appointed to the post of Secretary of State for Northern Ireland, a man called Merlyn Rees. Rees had visited the Long Kesh camp in 1971, soon after it had been set up, and he had been disgusted at the whole idea of internment without trial. Over the years since then, he had badgered the Conservative Northern Ireland Secretary, William Whitelaw, to give a date when internment would be ended. Now that he had himself assumed that post, he was determined to end what he saw as a shocking practice, as soon as was humanly possible.

Earlier in this chapter, the camp at Long Kesh was described as a 'concentration camp'. Some readers might have thought this to be a slight exaggeration, but the politicians themselves during those years were under no illusion at all about the essential nature of the camp. Speaking of his visit to Long Kesh, Merlyn Rees said years later:

I found the idea of a concentration camp offensive. For me personally, ending internment was something positive that I had done and it was the right thing to do. If all I have in history is a footnote saying, 'Merlyn Rees ended internment', that will satisfy me.

Here is a man who was a government Minister, using the term 'concentration camp' to describe a compound set up in the United kingdom and still operating until the end of 1975!

It is of course one thing to demand action from a government when you are still a member of the opposition; quite another to take that same action when you are yourself on the government front benches and in possession of all the facts. Despite all his rhetoric on the subject, it took the newly appointed Secretary of State for Northern Ireland almost two years to end internment without trial. There is an interesting modern parallel for Merlyn Rees' sluggishness on this.

Soon after he became President of the United States of America, Barack Obama promised to close down the detention centre at Guantanamo Bay, where suspected terrorists had been held without trial for years. That was in 2009. At the time of writing, in the spring of 2015; the camp remains open and there is no prospect of its being closed in the near-future. So it was with the decision to release the men being held without charge at the Long Kesh camp. Merlyn Rees was appointed to his post in March 1974, It was not until 24 July the following year that he announced plans to close the camp; promising that all the prisoners would be home for Christmas that year.

Over the autumn of 1975, detainees at Long Kesh and the other sites were released at regular intervals, until by the beginning of December; only forty-six remained. On Friday, 5 December 1975, the last internees were freed and Britain's last concentration camp became a prison containing only those men who had been brought before the courts and properly convicted. It was the end of seventy-five years of British use of camps to hold political prisoners and various ethnic minorities who were making a nuisance of themselves.

For the next few years, the government in London quietly retained the option to begin arresting people and holding them indefinitely without trial, should they feel the need to do so in the future. It was not until 9 July 1980 that the law which provided for internment was finally dropped. This marked the end of the United Kingdom's use of internment without trial.

Endword

We have in this book looked at the concept of concentration camps and examined the way in which they evolved over the course of the twentieth century. Far from being somehow associated with the excesses of the Third Reich, we have seen that concentration camps have been a part of British history from 1900 onwards. If any country justly deserves to have its name linked with the development and use of concentration camps; that nation is Britain, rather than Germany. Since the end of the Second World War and the revelation of the horrors of the Holocaust though, nobody has wanted to be seen making use of concentration camps and so the British have used a variety of euphemisms for such places; prisoner of war camps, internment camps and New Villages being some of these. Occasionally, the cat has been let out of the bag when a government Minister like Merlyn Rees casually refers to a 'concentration camp', but this has been rare. Whatever the name used, the essential purpose of the concentration camp has remained unchanged. They are used to gather together people whom a regime feels are its enemies or who might perhaps aid those enemies, in one convenient spot, where they can be supervised and observed. This is done without any of the tiresome restraints such as bringing people to trial or even allowing them access to courts. A disturbing aspect of the situations at which we have looked is that these supposed enemies of the regime have, in the case of the British, almost invariably been members of various ethnic groups: Jews, Chinese, Africans, Germans or Irish.

The British seem, since the freeing of their last political prisoners in 1975, to have fallen out of love with concentration camps. One only has to see the enormous fuss about holding terrorist suspects for twenty-eight days, a few years ago, the reverberations from which almost brought down a Prime Minister, to see how our views have changed over the last forty years, since the closing of the last British concentration camp. It is exceedingly unlikely that any future government of the United Kingdom will feel able to detain political prisoners or members of some ethnic minority without trial in the future; such are the sensitivities surrounding the matter. It is not only the expression 'concentration camp' which has now fallen from favour, but the very idea of holding people indefinitely without trial.

It is unlikely that many people will be found in this country who mourn the passing of British concentration camps; most would probably agree that such establishments have no place in the twenty-first century. All the indications are that they are likely to remain an historical curiosity.

Bibliography

Ayto, John (Editor) (2005), *Brewer's Dictionary of Phrase and Fable*, London, Wiedenfield & Nicolson

Bard, Mitchell G. (2002), *Myths and Facts: A Guide to the Arab-Israeli Conflict* Chevy Chase, American-Israel Cooperative Enterprise

Bennett, Huw (2012), *Fighting the Mau Mau: The British Army and Counter-Insurgency in the Kenya Emergency* Cambridge, Cambridge University Press

Brewer, Paul (2007), *The Chronicle of War*, London, Carlton Books

Bunyan, Tony (1976), *The Political Police in Britain* London, Julian Friedmann Publishers

Cannon, John (Editor) (1997), *The Oxford Companion to British History* Oxford, Oxford University Press

Cobain, Ian (2012), *Cruel Britannia; A Secret History of Torture*, London, Portobello Books

Edwards, Aaron (2011), *The Northern Ireland Troubles*, Newbury, Osprey

Elkins, Caroline (2005), *Britain's Gulag; The Brutal End of Empire in Kenya*, London, Pimlico

Frankland, Noble (Editor) (1989), *The Encyclopaedia of 20th Century Warfare*, London, Mitchell Beazley International

Garnett, Mark & Weight, Richard (2004), *Modern British History*, London, Pimlico

Gilbert, Martin (1997), *A History of the Twentieth Century*, London, HarperCollins

Gilbert, Martin (1998), *Descent into Barbarism*, London, HarperCollins

Hewitt, Peter (2008), *Kenya Cowboy: A Police Officer's Account of the Mau Mau Emergency*, London, 30 Degrees South Publishers

Isaacs, Jeremy & Downing, Taylor (1998), *The Cold War*, London, Transworld Publishers

Judd, Dennis & Surridge, Keith (2002), *The Boer War*, London, John Murray

Kee, Robert (1980), *Ireland: A History*, London, Wiedenfield & Nicolson

Mackay, James (1996), *Michael Collins: A Life*, Edinburgh, Mainstream Publishing

Mao Tse-Tung (1967), *Quotations from Chairman Mao Tse-Tung*, Peking, Foreign Language Press

McGuffin, John (1974), *The Guinea Pigs*, London, Penguin Books

Nasson, Bill (2010), *The Boer War*, Cape Town, NB Publishers

Packenham, Thomas (1991), *The Boer War*, London, Abacus

Panteli, Stavros (2003), *Place of refuge: A History of the Jews in Cyprus*, Elliot and Thompson

Prazmowska, Anita (1995), *Britain and Poland 1939-1943*, Cambridge, Cambridge University Press

Pretorius, Fran Johan (1985), *The Anglo-Boer War 1899-1902*, Cape Town, Don Nelson

Priestley, J.B. (1970), *The Edwardians*, London, William Heinemann

Rayner, Ed & Stapley, Ron (2002), *Debunking History*, Stroud, Sutton Publishing

Rees, Laurence (2005), *Auschwitz*, London, BBC Worldwide

Regan, Geoffrey (1991), *Military Blunders*, Enfield, Guinness Publishing

Robertson, Patrick (1974), *The Shell Book of Firsts*, London, Ebury Press

Roland, Paul (2012), *The Nuremberg Trials*, London, Arcturus Publishing

Segev, Tom (2001), *One Palestine, Complete: Jews and Arabs Under the British Mandate*, London, Abacus

Slee, Christopher (1994), *The Guinness Book of Lasts*, Enfield, Guinness Publishing

Watson, Jack (1974), *Twentieth Century World Affairs*, London, John Murray

Williams, Anne & Head, Vivian (2007), *Freedom Fighters*, London, Futura

Index